GOD OF HOPE

Donald Coggan was born in London in October 1909, and educated at Merchant Taylors' School, St John's College, Cambridge and Wycliffe Hall, Oxford.

In 1931 he became Assistant Lecturer in Semitic Languages and Literature at Manchester University, and three years later became curate of St Mary's Church, Islington. In 1937 he went to Canada, where he was professor at Wycliffe College, Toronto, returning to England in 1944 to become Principal of the London College of Divinity. In 1956 he became Bishop of Bradford, and later Archbishop of York (1961–74).

In 1974 Dr Coggan became the one hundred and first Archbishop of Canterbury, a position he held until 1980.

His leisure interests include gardening, motoring and music, and he is the author of numerous books, including *The Heart of the Christian Faith* and *The Sacrament of the Word* (both also published by Fount Paperbacks), *Cuthbert Bardsley: Bishop, Evangelist, Pastor* (Collins 1989), and *Paul: Portrait of a Revolutionary* (Hodder 1984). His wife, Jean, is an author in her own right. The Coggans have two grown-up daughters.

*Books by the same author
available from HarperCollinsReligious
in the Fount imprint*

Cuthbert Bardsley (Hardback)
The Sacrament of the Word (Paperback)

For Ann
who trains young hopefuls

Donald Coggan

GOD OF HOPE

A BIBLE STUDY
AND A COMMENT

Fount
An Imprint of HarperCollins*Publishers*

First published in Great Britain
in 1991 by Fount Paperbacks

Fount Paperbacks is an imprint of
HarperCollinsReligious
Part of HarperCollinsPublishers
77–85 Fulham Palace Road, London W6 8JB

Phototypeset by Intype, London
Printed and bound in Great Britain
by HarperCollins Manufacturing, Glasgow

Contents

Foreword

Scott of the Antarctic, at the end of his last expedition, as he lay in his tent facing death, wrote of Edward Wilson, his great companion in adversity, lying there beside him: "His eyes have a comfortable blue look of hope."

These words at once conjure up for me the faces of others who seem to encourage us all on our journeys. Such people have some kind of family likeness about them, a common spiritual trait. Lord Coggan, himself, is undoubtedly of that special company. It is thus extraordinarily fitting that he should have taken up in this book of exposition, and encouragement to prayer, the theme of biblical hope.

This is a theme which, as the book makes clear, touches our society at one of its sorest points. It lifts us beyond some of the sadly illusory hopes of our contemporary world and even of parts of the contemporary Church. But, even more to the point, it breaks through so much of the scepticism and relativism of our present culture, seemingly so knowing, but in reality often so profoundly confused and empty.

One of the striking illustrations in the fourth chapter, as it reflects on the implications of the biblical message for today, is a song from a recent musical called, characteristically, *Lost in the Stars*. The song compares human life to the flight of a bird through a lighted room, coming out of the night through an open door and going out again into the dark:

> Out of darkness we come at birth
> Into a lamp-lit room, and then –
> Go forward into dark again,
> Go forward into dark again.

It is startling perhaps to realize that this is not a newly coined contemporary image, but ancient. It was used at the dawning of Christian faith in the dark ages, in the Anglo-Saxon world in the seventh century. It is there in Bede's *History of the English Church and People* (Bk. II: ch. 13). At the court of King Edwin of Northumbria, when Bishop Paulinus had presented the Gospel, one of the King's chief men supported the argument of the High Priest of the old religion that they should accept the new message. He used precisely the same comparison of our life to the swift flight of a lone sparrow through the King's banqueting hall in winter-time out of the storms of snow and rain, through one door of the hall, past the comforting fire, and out again through another door. "Therefore if this new teaching can reveal any more certain knowledge it seems only right to follow it."

We appear to be back at the beginning again. We have come to a time when, once more, all religions and philosophies (including now some forms of Christianity itself) seem broken and uncertain. Once more the biblical message of God with us and for us, drawing us firmly into participating in the mystery of Christ's death and resurrection, offers the one real hope, so lucidly set forth in these pages.

May those who take this little book to guide them, either in personal or in group study and, above all, in prayer, be made, like the book's author himself, into clear and purposeful messengers of hope in our own dark age. And may the book itself be mightily used to give, and to spread amongst many, firm grounds for hope in this Decade of Evangelism, laying a good foundation for the century to come.

†*SIMON COVENTRY*
January 1991

Introduction

Let us imagine that the year is 2000. An historian is at his desk. He is attempting, in a few pages, to describe the main marks of the history of mankind during the twentieth century. His task is complex and demanding. But certain features would stand out clearly.

He would note that the century saw an advance in knowledge far greater than that of any comparable period in the preceding two millennia. The conquest of space through air travel; the landing on the moon; the arrival and development of radio and tele-communication, of the computer, of the micro-chip, of Fax; the splitting of the atom; the advance of medical science and of psychological and psychiatric research; the easing of the pain of mankind; the care of the social services; the availability of knowledge to all classes through the burgeoning of universities and colleges. . . . **Progress** on many fronts: this he would need to elaborate.

Change would stand out for comment. Our historian would note that the political world map of 1900 was almost unrecognizable in 2000. The British Empire had gone. The European monarchies had disappeared. Communist domination had risen – only to fall. Africa, after long periods of Western exploration and rule, and after many convulsions, was taking on again a life of its own. Latin America was exhibiting possibilities of development unglimpsed before. China and Japan were flexing their muscles as world powers, bidding fair to take over from the West.

Violence had been rampant. A series of wars, world wars and "local" wars, had been all the more terrible because science had made available weapons of unimaginable horror. Violence on the streets of our cities had increased. The violence of disease had shown itself in many forms – there were conquests to record but also new forms of sickness to be faced, some strangely resistant to all attempts to eradicate them.

So our historian would go on. Progress, change, violence – and many other features – would await his describing. But it is likely that, above all and through all, he would note a change of **mood**.

The twentieth century opened with a note of confidence amounting almost to euphoria. The aged Queen Victoria seemed in herself to be a symbol of stability. Man was "coming of age" (even if that phrase was only to become popular later in the century). Utopia was round the corner – given a little more knowledge and we would arrive (precisely where was not always made clear). Who could stop human progress? Man was the master of things.

Who was to envisage the ravages of war, the fury of Communism, the fall of the idols, and the vacuum which was to follow the toppling of man's gods? Who was to tame man's rapacity – his rape of Nature, his spoliation of forests, lakes, air? Who was to answer his cry: "Let me eat and drink, for tomorrow I die – and there is nothing beyond. Give it me, and give it me *now*"? Who was to fill his vacuum? Was there an answer for T. S. Eliot's "hollow men ... the stuffed men leaning together", for whom "the world ends not with a bang but a whimper"?

I believe our historian would find himself compelled to describe the mood of the latter part of the twentieth century in terms of disillusion, even of despair and of hopelessness. Why had mankind, advancing so rapidly in learning and discovery, proved unable to break the power of hate, to resolve international differences by other means than war, to overcome the problems presented by barriers of race and sex and the folly of the arms race? Why had so many thoughtful people felt bound to abandon belief in human progress? What content could be put into the word "hope"? Perhaps it should be jettisoned from our vocabulary. . . ?

The results of such disillusion are to be seen in an uncertainty about the worthwhileness of life and endeavour; a hesitation of step and direction; a dissipation of energy; a tendency to lurch rather than to march along life's road.

If our historian was familiar with the world of the first century as well as that of the twentieth, he might very well find himself tracing certain interesting parallels between the two. There were contrasts, of course. The *pax Romana* of those long past days contrasts with the convulsions of our own century, the *lingua franca* of Greek with the competing claims of German, Spanish, English, Japanese today. But the parallels are more striking, the fall of the gods not least. Paul, as he travelled that world, found it full of gods – but they were *fallen* gods, not to be trusted by intelligent men and women.

Wistfully people were looking towards the monotheism of Judaism and to its high ethical ideals. The pagan gods had proved to be no-gods, so that the writer of the Epistle to the Ephesians could describe his world as "a world without hope and without God" (2:12). The juxtaposition of those two concepts is highly significant. When God is abandoned, or when the gods are proved inadequate, the result is soon seen in a bankruptcy not only of belief but also of morals, of stamina, of hope. There is a terrible intimacy between the concept of god-lessness and hopelessness.

As then, so now. As in the first century, so in the twentieth. Our historian could develop an interesting theme.

The parallel has been much in my mind as I have striven, over a long period, to write this little book. In an age of disillusion, even of despair, what has the Christian Church to say? Has it, in any realistic sense, a word of hope to offer? I believe it has. All too often that note has been muted if not silenced. It is time we took it out of the Christian treasury and looked at it anew – not in expectation of an easy answer to all our problems, but as a neglected part of our heritage.

Paul, in giving us the great trio "faith, hope and love, these three", assured us that "the greatest of these is love" (1 Corinthians 13:13). True. Perhaps if he were here today, he might add: "The most neglected of these is hope." Look at any well-stocked theological library, and you will find the shelves full of books on faith and love, but thin in their supply of books on hope. There are, of course, splendid exceptions – one has only to mention the contributions of Jürgen Moltmann, John

Macquarrie and Walter Brueggemann, to name only three contemporary writers. In the Bible, however, hope is a major theme.

In writing this book, I have had in mind the **individual** who wishes to come to grips with the concept, and the **group** whose members want to engage in a joint study. To both individual and group I would suggest that the best way to begin would be to read the biblical part (chapters 1–3) straight through, reasonably slowly but not delaying to look up references. That will give the reader(s) the opportunity to understand the general thrust of the book.

Then will come the time to return to those chapters for a more leisurely study – how leisurely is for the individual or the group members to say. Some may find it adequate simply to turn up and ponder the references given to a particular biblical writer (for example, to Jeremiah (pp. 21–22), or to Habakkuk (pp. 24–25), or to Jesus (pp. 38ff.), or to Paul (pp. 50ff.)). Others may find that these references will set them off on a voyage of discovery and they will want to linger on a more careful study of some particular writer. That would be all to the good. Let each reader or group find their own *tempo*.

The biblical chapters constitute an invitation to dig, to explore. Such work cannot be done in a hurry; but the reader who is prepared to delay, to wait, to "chew the cud", will be richly rewarded. For, as we shall see, the Hebrew word for "hope" means to wait on, to look expectantly to. When a person waits on God, looks expectantly and confidently to the God and Father of our Lord Jesus Christ, he has within him the basis for a hope which cannot be shaken. It is by "the encouragement" given by the scriptures that "we maintain our hope with perseverance" (Romans 15:4).

It will be at once apparent that there is a hemisphere of difference between biblical hope and the way that the word "hope" is used in everyday conversation. In today's English, "hope" is a poor thing. It has undergone a process of evisceration (the *Collins English Dictionary* defines "eviscerate" as "remove the internal organs of"; so "deprive of meaning or significance"). "I hope" often means little more than "I would like to think that . . . , but it is very unlikely to happen." In contrast, we shall notice that in the biblical writings, "hope" and "faith" are very close cousins. One could wish that we might call a moratorium on the use of the word "hope", and substitute something like "expectancy" in its place. There is a touch of the tiptoe about the "hope" of the Bible. It is a lively concept.

Chapters 4 and 5 seek to relate the findings of the Bible studies to life as it is in the Church and in contemporary society. What does it mean to have no hope or to have an ill-grounded hope? Wherein does the Christian hope differ from hopes offered elsewhere? Can we say with honesty and realism: "All my hope on God is founded"? What does it mean to be a messenger of hope?

Since all Bible study should issue in prayer, thirty-one prayers of hope will be found at the end of the book, one for each day of the month if so be the reader thinks that is the best way to use them.

The Scripture references are almost always taken from the *Revised English Bible (1989)*.

Introduction

I am most grateful to Simon Barrington-Ward, Bishop of Coventry, an old and valued friend, for his kindness in writing the Foreword, and to Armorel and Philip Willmot for their skill and patience in deciphering my manuscript and preparing the book for the press.

Donald Coggan
Winchester

The Conversion of St Paul
1991

BIBLE STUDY

To cherish a hope . . . is . . . to embrace that which is difficult but possible to attain – possible because there is a righteous God at work in the world. It is this God himself who is the "hope of Israel".

John Macquarrie,
Christian Hope, p. 37

1

The Birth of Hope

The library of books which we call the Bible is a library of hope. Its writers – perhaps we should exclude the unknown author of Ecclesiastes! – were all men of hope. They were not facile optimists – far from it. Many of them – most of them – knew the meaning of trial, grief, pain, doubt, at first hand. They were down-to-earth realists. Often they cried to God "out of the depths" and those depths led sometimes to the brink of despair. *But* they were men of hope.

Here is a phenomenon worth examining. It will be a useful task at least to try to find the key to its understanding.

Abraham has become to later generations the quintessential man of faith, the father of the faithful, his faith "counted to him for righteousness" (Romans 4; Hebrews 11:8–10, 17–19). But he could equally validly be called the man of *hope*. Indeed, Paul makes the point: it was "when hope seemed hopeless" that "his faith was such that he became 'father of many nations' " (Romans 4:18). For "looking forward to a city with firm foundations, whose architect and builder is God", the man of faith proved himself to be the man of hope.

Nor, from the viewpoint of the writer of Genesis, was Abraham the first to hope when all others were nigh to despair. The old story of Noah introduces us to a man of hope who, when all the earth seemed ripe for destruction, dared to build an ark in obedience to the word that came from God. So firm was his hope, that he set out to re-start a civilization, convinced that "as long as the earth lasts, seedtime and harvest, cold and heat, summer and winter, day and night, they will never cease" (Genesis 8:22).

The story of the exodus, which centuries later was to become the paradigm for the story of Christ's rescue of God's people from the tyranny of sin and death, is the story *par excellence* of the triumph of hope over despair. For centuries around their camp-fires the Jewish people loved to recount stories of the depths from which their people had been rescued, depths of slavery, watery depths with pursuing Egyptians, depths of despair. But when hope seemed hopeless, they held on, and God in his mercy did his act of deliverance. The ordeal was long drawn out. The grumblings and the longings for the life back in Egypt recurred again and again. Even Moses, the great leader, was halted on the brink of the promised land. But Joshua saw the people in. Hope was rewarded. Even the valley of Achor, the stony and troubled place where Achan and his family met their fearful end (Joshua 7:24–26), would be turned "into a gate of hope" (Hosea 2:15), "a pasture for cattle" (Isaiah 65:10).

It is when we reach the Hebrew prophets that the theme of hope comes into its own in a majestic way.

Walter Brueggemann was, until recently, Professor of Old Testament at Columbia Theological Seminary in Atlanta, Georgia. In his *Hopeful Imagination: Prophetic*

Voices in Exile (Fortress Press, Philadelphia, 1986) he has given us a book of great importance. It is a study of those prophets, Jeremiah, Ezekiel, and 2 Isaiah (chapters 40ff.), men who gave us "some of the boldest and most eloquent theological probing in the Old Testament" (p.1). They all three wrote at a period when the old world-order of the Jewish people, centred in Jerusalem and in temple worship, was breaking up. Babylon was expanding its borders; Israel was in exile. Most of the people despaired. But the prophets, with the vision of poets, penetrated the clouds of despair and, in the darkest hours, dared to hope that in spite of the destruction of the temple and its worship, God was able and longing to do a *new* thing.

Even **Jeremiah**, whose name has long stood for "a person who habitually prophesies doom or denounces contemporary society" (*Collins English Dictionary*) is essentially a poet-prophet of hope. True, his long prophecy introduces the reader to a man of conflict – conflict with his neighbours, conflict with himself, and, not least, conflict with his God. Who but a bold realist would venture to accuse his God of having "duped" him (20:7), unless he was a flippant blasphemer, which Jeremiah most certainly was not? The book "speaks harsh judgement and inescapable destruction, but it also articulates passionate hope" (p.10). The commission which is given Jeremiah from the Lord is in terms of uprooting and pulling down, of destroying and demolishing, but it is given also, and in the same breath, in terms of building and planting (1:10). The people may be in exile, groaning under a foreign yoke, but Jeremiah hears God saying, "I alone know my purpose for you, says the

Lord: wellbeing and not misfortune, and a long line of descendants after you" (29:11). Grief, deep grief, is at the heart of this prophecy; the sorrow is poignant. But grief is the soil out of which hope springs – Jeremiah saw that, and Paul gave words to it: "suffering is a source of endurance, endurance of approval, and approval of hope. Such hope is no fantasy" (Romans 5:3–5). Out of the hurt of the Babylonian exile, there is the possibility of *newness*. Jeremiah posits the question: can his hearers (readers) see that the hope of the future lies not in a re-building of an old institution but in the re-birth of faith in the living God?

Ezekiel, tough and "relentless about the holiness of God" (p.61), concerned to "let God have God's relentless way" (p.63), convinced that his supreme task was to warn his community of coming danger, to be a watchman in the night, sitting where his people sat in gloomy exile by the river Kebar (1:1), sometimes struck dumb with no word to utter (3:26), bereft of his beloved wife (24:15ff.) – this stern, smitten poet-prophet, too, is a man of hope. The scattered bones will yet come together, winds will come from every quarter and dry bones will come to life – "you will know that I the Lord have spoken and I shall act. This is the word of the Lord" (37:1–14).

Second **Isaiah** (chapters 40–55) is "buoyant literature of hope exquisitely expressed" (p.90). The Babylonian empire under Nebuchadnezzar is passing, the Persian empire under Cyrus is rising. Nations are heaving like the waves of the sea. But God can use the pagan Nebuchadnezzar or Cyrus as his agent, as his very Messiah, in the outworking of his purpose. There will be a homecoming for his people whose "term of bondage is served, her penalty paid" (40:2). The Babylonian gods will be seen for what they actually are – unable to speak or act, unable to carry anyone, able only themselves to be carried (46:1,2). The poet-prophet's God, by contrast, is a God whose word gets things done, never returning to him empty without accomplishing his purpose, always succeeding in the task for which he sent it (55:11). "The grass" of Babylonian pretensions "may wither, the flower fade, but the word of our God will endure for ever" (40:8). God's purposes may ripen slowly or rapidly, but they will ripen; his sovereign plan will prevail.

No wonder that these poet-prophets of hope found the metaphor of the *watchman* a congenial one. Each of these major prophets to whom we have just referred uses the metaphor.

Jeremiah depicts God appointing watchmen to direct the people and bidding them listen for the trumpet-call. But they said: "We refuse" (6:17). And in a more cheerful passage, he sees in anticipation the day "when the watchmen cry on Ephraim's hills, 'come, let us go up to Zion, to the Lord our God' " (31:6).

Ezekiel, after a period with the exiles at Tel-abib "in a state of consternation", at last hears the word of the Lord: "I have appointed you, O man, a watchman for the Israelites; you will pass to them the warnings you receive from me" (3:16–17). The theme is elaborated in a passage about responsibility – the onus is on the prophet-spokesman to deliver the message, and on the people to receive the word of warning.

Isaiah is bidden: "Go, post a watchman to report what he sees." Then he hears someone calling to him:

"Watchman, what is left of the night? Watchman, what is left of it?" The answer is ambiguous, unwelcome: "Morning comes, and so does night. Come back again and ask if you will" (21:6,11,12). A watchman's task is beset with perplexity; there is not always clear vision. But sometimes he is rewarded. Sometimes the watchmen "raise their voices and shout together in joy; for with their own eyes they see the Lord return to Zion" (52:8). There can be, and sometimes are, pseudo-watchmen, "blind, with no powers of perception, dumb, loving their sleep, greedy, understanding nothing, intent on their own gain" (56:10–12). Their presence makes the task of the *true* watchman all the more essential.

The minor prophets also find the metaphor of the watchman congenial. **Hosea** complains that "God appointed the prophet as a watchman for Ephraim, but he has become a fowler's trap on all their ways. There is enmity in the very temple of God" (9:8).

In the brave little prophecy of **Habakkuk** we can see the Lord's watchman at work. The book opens with a passionate, even furious, protest to God – "How long, Lord, will you be deaf to my plea? 'Violence!' I cry out to you, but you do not come to the rescue." Here is the problem of a God immortal (v.12) but apparently inactive while "that savage and impetuous nation", the Chaldeans, "march far and wide over the earth to seize and occupy what is not theirs". Maybe they are God's agents "to execute judgement, commissioned to punish" (v.12). But why this silence, these brazen heavens, while the wicked make merry? Where is God in all this inhuman pitilessness? (vv.12–17).

The storm of protest subsides. The prophet decides

what to do. He will do nothing – as men conceive inactivity. There shall be a time of silent waiting, an attitude of expectancy. "I shall stand at my post, I shall take up my position on the watchtower, keeping a look-out to learn what he says to me, how he responds to my complaint" (2:1). All that he can do is to be on the alert, open to the unpredictable, receptive to the new. And the answer to his openness came. "The Lord gives me the answer: Write down a vision, inscribe it clearly on tablets, so that it may be read at a glance. There *is* still a vision for the appointed time . . . though it delays, wait for it, for it will surely come before too long" (2:2,3).

The task of the watchman is never an easy one. The loftier his concept of the holiness and the justice of his God, the greater becomes the problem of man's inhumanity to man, and the more agonized the prophet's "why?" Maybe there would be a delay before the problems presented by a bully-nation began to make some sense, but "the righteous will live by *being faithful*" (2:4). Standing at his post, keeping a look-out over the terrors of contemporary events and a look-up to God, there grew in the prophet an inner confidence that justice and truth must prevail, even though in the short term it often did not do so. He lived in a barren period of history, and the prospect was, humanly speaking, bleak. "The fig tree has no buds, the vine bears no harvest, the olive crop fails, the orchards yield no food, the fold is bereft of its flock, and there are no cattle in the stalls. *Even so* I shall exult in the Lord and rejoice in the God who saves me. The Lord God is my strength . . ." (3:17–19).

God of Hope

The Old Testament writers have much to say about hope, about looking (expectantly) to God, about waiting on God. There is one major word which covers all these ideas and which is variously translated in our English renderings. It is the word *qiwwah*. The basic notion of the word, so the Hebrew scholars tell us, is that of tension (as of a rope stretched, or a string of a musical instrument). In this word there is a tone of tense anticipation and confidence, attention born of commitment to the proposition that justice and truth must prevail though in the short term it does not always do so or appear to do so.

We have already touched on the powerful hope which enabled the writer of Isaiah 40 and the following chapters to have confidence in God in the midst of a rocking civilization. In a passage of great power (40:21–31) he paints a picture of the mighty Creator, enthroned on the vaulted roof of the world, stretching out the skies like a curtain, leading out their host one by one and summoning each by name, the Lord, the eternal God who does not weary or grow faint. Then, at the close of the chapter, the prophet turns from the picture of the mighty God to that of frail humanity, the weary, the exhausted (vv.29–31). "Young men may grow weary and faint, even the fittest may stumble and fall; but *those who look to the Lord* . . ." Here is the dominant word, the word of quiet waiting, of tense and confident anticipation. Here is the secret of vigour and of new strength (vv.29,31). The prophet spells it out in three graphic pictures – the eagle, soaring into the eye of the sun; the runner in a gruelling marathon; the walker, perhaps a soldier, slogging it out mile after mile. There is excitement in the concept of the eagle in flight, and in that of the athlete in his race. There is little of the dramatic in marching with a pack on your back and blisters on your feet. The eagle, the runner, the slogger – all need an infusion of strength. It comes, says the prophet, to those who *look to*, wait on the God who, himself never weary or faint, shares his own vigour with them.

It has been said that there are two ways of destroying a person: one is to give him no hope; the other is to give him a false hope. The first needs little elaboration – we have only to think of friends of our own who, on retiring, have nothing to look forward to, nothing to engage their powers. We have watched their rapid decline.

But the danger of having a false hope is far more subtle and even more perilous. It constitutes a major theme in the Old Testament and the prophets made much of it. These men of keen spiritual insight poured scorn on those who sought to go for their help to Egypt, that ill-omened place of servitude and bondage. "Woe betide the rebellious children!" he hears the Lord say. "Without consulting me they hurry down to Egypt to seek shelter under Pharaoh's protection, to take refuge under Egypt's shadow . . . that unprofitable nation will leave everyone in sorry plight; they will find neither help nor profit, only humiliation and contempt" (Isaiah 30:1–5).

That same prophet clearly appreciates the sarcasm with which Sennacherib's chief officer taunts King Hezekiah if the latter should be foolish enough to rely on Egypt's support in rebelling against "the Great King, the king of Assyria: 'On whom do you rely for support in your rebellion against me? On Egypt? Egypt is a splintered cane that will run into a man's hand and pierce it if he leans on it. That is what Pharaoh king of Egypt proves to all who rely on him' " (Isaiah 36:4ff.). In similar vein, the prophet utters his anathema on "those who go down to Egypt for help and rely on horses, who put their trust in chariots because they are many, and in horsemen because of their vast numbers, but do not *look to* the Holy One of Israel or seek guidance of the Lord" (31:1). The supreme apostasy is horizontal hope when it should be vertical; secular hope when it should be religious. The arm of flesh is bound to fail.

Like the prophets, the Psalmists make much of hoping in God, looking to God, waiting on God. Often, they spoke out of the depths of their experience of the futility of horizontal hope, of putting any expectation in frail humanity. Could their trust and hope be transferred to a surer ground of confidence? Was *that* the way of true religion, of life as its Giver meant it to be? We look at a few instances:

The author of Psalm 37 is, clearly, a man of marked spirituality. He knows what it is to "trust in the Lord" (v.3), to "delight in the Lord" (v.4), to "commit" his "way to the Lord" (v.5), to "wait quietly for the Lord" and to "be patient till he comes" (v.7). The secret of a life lived in this way is developed in v.9. It is for those who *hope* in the Lord. Given that relationship to God, there is no reason for vexation and envy (v.1), for fuss and worry. The tornado may rage, but in the eye of the storm is a place of calm where the Lord is. As the writer of Psalm 25 puts it: "No one whose *hope* is in you is put to shame . . . you are God my saviour; in you I put my *hope* all day long" (vv.3,5).

The author of Psalm 40 is clearly a man of action. He is concerned with the public proclamation of God's deeds and purposes – "I would proclaim them and speak of them, but they are more than I can tell" (v.5); "I have proclaimed your faithfulness and saving power, and have not concealed your unfailing love and truth from the great assembly" (v.10). He is concerned with the ethical implications of religious belief (v.9). With God's law in his heart, his great desire is to do the will of God (v.8). We may ask: where does this man of action find his motive power for public work and private devotion? We note how the psalm begins – "patiently I *waited* for the Lord" (v.1, the verb is the same as the one we have been considering above: *qiwwah*). The *New English Bible* reflects the Hebrew more literally than does the *Revised English Bible* – "I waited, waited for the Lord". It is clear that this patient, expectant waiting did not go unrewarded. On the contrary, it was the prelude to a great discovery about God, the God who discloses his nature in and through his manifold activity, going out to meet the Psalmist in his need – "he bent down . . . listened . . . raised me . . . set my feet on rock . . . gave me a firm footing . . . on my lips he put a new song" (vv.1–3). The Psalmist proved that time spent in waiting on God, in looking expectantly to him, is never wasted. It is at once the key to vision into the nature of God and the source of power for activity in the world.

The author of Psalm 62 makes clear the close association between an experience of God as a rock of deliverance, his strong tower, a rock of refuge and a shelter (vv.6,7) and an attitude of waiting silently on that God – "for God alone I wait silently; my deliverance comes from him" (v.1 cf. v.5 "for God alone I wait silently; my hope comes from him"). The Psalmist's confident expectancy is grounded in the granite of God's essential being.

Psalm 130 presents us with a man not concerned with public duty and activity (as was the author of Psalm 40), but with his own sins and shortcomings. He cries out to God from the depths of conviction of sin. What is to be done when a sinful man faces a holy God? "Who could hold his ground?" (v.3). He answers his own question. He will wait – wait eagerly; he will hope expectantly – longingly (vv.5,6). So he finds a God whose love is unfailing, whose power to deliver is great, in whose heart is forgiveness (vv.4,7,8).

His use of the picture of the watchman is delightful. The Psalmist knew nothing of electric light! The darkness of the night spelt fear and aprehension in streets and homes. The shutting of the town's gates was but a poor defence against the attack under darkness of enemy forces. It was the task of the watchman from his vantage-point to be on the alert – and how he longed for the first streaks of dawn, for the coming of the light which scattered fear and established confidence! "My soul waits for the Lord more eagerly than watchmen for the morning. . . ."

From what has been said above, it is clear that for a Hebrew writer to "wait on God" was not to lapse into a state of passivity. There was much more to it than that! To wait is to be *willing*. The word "expectancy" which we have used implies some action on God's part; but it involves also a willingness, even a desire and longing, to respond when God reveals his will. To wait is not to lapse into inactivity. It is to be ready to engage in action when God shows that the time for action is ripe.

It has been a moving exercise to watch these Old Testament men of hope – Noah, Abraham, prophets, psalmists – wrestling with the facts of life within them and around them and working out and maintaining a hope centred in their faithful God. The exercise is all the more moving when one comes to terms with the fact that this hope was, for almost all the Old Testament writers, a hope which did not transcend the bounds of this brief life. That statement demands some qualifying, in as much as some of these men of hope dared to believe that their hope in God would find its fruition if not in their own lifetime then in that of their descendants. But it was a this-worldly hope; it did not breach the bounds of eternity. The hope of an afterlife in anything like the form in which later Christian generations were to conceive it was almost unknown to these people.

To die was to go down into Sheol, a region of shadows and futility, a place of silence and forgetting, the grave, the pit. "Hear my prayer, Lord; listen to my cry", pleads the Psalmist. "Do not be deaf to my weeping, for I find shelter with you; I am a passing guest, as all my forefathers were. Frown on me no more; let me look cheerful before I depart and cease to be" (Psalm 39:12,13). There is a stark contrast delineated in Psalm 115 – "It is not the dead who praise the Lord, not those who go down to the silent grave; but we, the living, shall bless the Lord now and for evermore" (vv.17,18). "Among the dead no one remembers you", the Psalmist cries out to God; "in Sheol who praises you?" (6:5). "Will it be for the dead you work wonders? Or can the shades rise up and praise you? . . . Will your wonders be known in the region of darkness, your victories in the land of oblivion?" (88:10,12). The answer to these questions, though not expressed, is clearly "No". The abyss, the pit, the place of shades, of silence, from it there is no rescue (89:48), in it dust can no longer praise the Creator nor proclaim his truth (30:9).

When King Hezekiah learned that he was mortally ill, he "turned his face to the wall" and wept. As one reads the story (Isaiah 38) one senses the intensity of his relief when he was granted a remission of fifteen years. There was a terrible finality linked with human physical frailty. "Consigned to the gates of Sheol", he would "no longer see the Lord as I did in the land of the living; I shall no longer see my fellow men as I did when I lived in the world" (vv.10ff.).

The most pathetic instance within the canon of the Old Testament of the absence of a doctrine of the after-life is to be found in the book of Ecclesiastes. "Futility, utter futility, says the Speaker, everything is futile" (1:2). Life lived totally within the limits of the temporal resulted in an extreme hopelessness, even an extreme cynicism. "Futility" rings like a death-knell through the book.

In Hosea 6:1–6 (a passage appointed for reading at Morning Prayer on Easter Eve), it is very doubtful whether there is a reference to a future life. "After two days he will revive us, on the third day he will raise us to life in his presence" is, much more probably, a poet's way of envisaging a renewed spiritual life in the very near future, consequent upon the people's "return to the Lord"; healing and restoration are round the corner.

It is generally agreed that the expectation of resurrection, clearly outlined in Daniel 12:2 ("many of those who sleep in the dust of the earth will awake, some to everlasting life and some to the reproach of eternal abhorrence") is from a very late book and belongs to that group of writings which are called "apocryphal".

We called the book of Habakkuk a "brave little prophecy" (p.24), for it "opens with a passionate, even furious, protest to God – 'How long, Lord, will you be deaf to my plea?' " Habakkuk was by no means the only devout man in the Old Testament to raise his voice in protest against the ways of God with men. If Habakkuk accuses God of deafness, the Psalmists accuse him of drowsiness – "Rouse yourself, Lord; why do you sleep? Awake! Do not reject us for ever" (44:23). "Awake, rouse yourself, my God, my Lord, to vindicate me and plead my cause" (35:23). Instances could be multiplied: the Psalms are peppered with outcries which, if it were not for their utter reality, would be outrageous if not blasphemous. And the book of Job – we have heard of his endurance and of "how he stood firm" (James 5:11), but surely *never* of his patience! For the whole poem is a protest of his innocence in the face of appalling injustice. It is a poem of moral outrage with a blasphemy which is cathartic. Why? Why? Why?

Why, if the prophets and the saints were right in saying that in heaven there is a God of love and of justice, why do the wicked prosper? To say that "a thousand may fall at your side, ten thousand close at hand, but you it will not touch" (Psalm 91:7) was too facile an answer to life's problems. In a war, bullets do not generally get diverted from the godly soldier and land only in the breasts of the ungodly! It became all too apparent that it was mighty hard, if not impossible, to work out a *theodicy*, a justification of the ways of God with men, if that search was to be limited to this world alone.

The problem would not go away. God's in his heaven; all is *not* right with his world. The protests continued and reached their climax in the years when the books of the Apocrypha came to be written, the years of what is generally, though inaccurately, called the inter-testament period. It was in those years that there was a fearful outbreak of anti-semitism, that curse which has haunted the people of Israel down the centuries. It seemed that the paganism of the vast world-powers – Persia, Greece, Rome – was successively unleashed against the purity of Israel's faith. The insidious attacks of polytheism, the immoralities of peoples who owed no allegiance to the ethics of the ten commandments, and then the sheer naked persecution of a "chosen" people who would rather die than conform to current patterns of belief and conduct – these things led to a head-on collision of faith. *If* the prophets were right that the God of Israel is the God of truth and justice, where was he in all this? (The modern form of the question is: "Where was God at Auschwitz?") If he was not rescuing his people in this life – and multitudes of them went to their deaths because of their faith – must there not be an afterlife, a judgement to come, beyond the boundaries of this tangible world? The members of this little beleaguered people clung on to their faith, to their sorely battered hope. *One day* – when, they could not say – God would act in justice and requital. *One day* he would come. *One day*, he would act and he would, in very fact, reign. So, sometimes in pretty crude forms, there began to emerge an eschatology, a doctrine of the "last things" or, would it be better to say, of "a coming One" before whom mankind would be arraigned. There would be a heaven. And there would be a hell. The terms in which that idea was expressed varied, but central was the concept of a putting to rights of the iniquities and inequities by which the purity of the pages of history have been stained. The very character of God demanded some such belief. It emerged from the demand for a *theodicy*, a justification of the ways of God with men.

The nobler members of Israel, and not least those who gave birth to the great Pharisaic movement, lit that eschatological hope and fanned its flame in the darkest days of their persecution. Like Abraham before them, "when hope seemed hopeless", they bravely hoped on. God was not dead. He would intervene. A day was coming. Expectancy was in the air.

Expectancy – yes. But expectancy of what? Of whom? That was the question which presented itself to the religious thinkers of Israel with a kind of nagging persistency. Would the expectancy be fulfilled in the person of a king on the model of their old hero David – one who would drive the oppressor into the sea, and reign in justice? Would they, or their descendants, see the ascendancy restored to David's house? Even after the resurrection of Jesus, so the writer of Acts tells us, there were those who asked the Lord whether this was the time when he was to restore sovereignty to Israel (1:6). Or was the expectancy to be fulfilled in a deeper sense than that of mere national liberation? Was there to be a radical re-specification of hope in terms only dimly glimpsed previously? There were people of a spiritual and thoughtful turn of mind who looked for one who would loose his people from a bondage more subtle and more enthralling than that of a national invader. Might he come in the form of a suffering-servant, with "no beauty, no majesty to catch our eyes, no grace to attract us to him ... despised, shunned by all, pain-racked and afflicted by disease ... pierced for our transgressions, crushed for our iniquities ... stricken to death for my people's transgression ... bearing the sin of many and interceding for transgressors" (Isaiah 53)? Might he come as "a little baby thing that made a woman cry"? It would take the spirituality of that "very old woman", Anna, to recognize in the Baby in the Temple the one who was to "liberate Jerusalem"; it would take the insight of old Simeon to perceive in that tiny child "a light that will bring revelation to the Gentiles and glory to your people Israel"(Luke 2:25ff.). But so it was, in the merciful and inscrutable counsels of God.

When *that* happened, "hope" came into its own. Its lineaments were clearer; its parameters wider; its outreach more glorious. To the New Testament we may now turn.

Lord of all hopefulness, Lord of all
joy. . .

Jan Struther

2

Jesus the Man of Hope

The people to whom Jesus came were a subject people. That is easy to write; difficult to imagine; bitter to endure. Their subjection to the Roman yoke led to sharp clashes between the Romans and a people whom they found it hard to understand: Why this hatred of anything which savoured of polytheism? Why this extraordinary sacrificial system centred in the Temple? Why this fanatical observance of a seventh-day rest? Why this suspicion, if not hatred, of the Emperor and all his works? The Romans found the Jews a people difficult to handle.

For their part, the Jews groaned under the tyranny of a pagan invasion which showed little respect for the land which was so dear to them; which sometimes rode roughshod over the things which were theirs by sacred inheritance; which imposed taxes grievous to be borne – the catalogue of complaints went on and on. Perhaps only those who have endured the take-over of their country by a foreign power can enter into the meaning of subjection to an enemy invader. Life at its best was drab; at its worst full of bitterness and despair. Hope, if it existed, was in short supply.

Into this little world Jesus came, fresh from his baptism, steeled by his temptation. Young – he was about thirty years of age, so St Luke tells us; greatly gifted – "never man spoke like this man", they said, as they listened to the words which stung and healed; deeply compassionate, with hands that brought recovery and life to the sick. His coming was like an eruption of fresh air into a fetid room, an injection of hope into a despairing community. "Jesus, Man of Hope", is an accurate description when we look at the evidence provided by the writers of the Gospels.

It would seem that he frequently accompanied his *acts* with the positive cry, "cheer up, have courage" (*tharsei*) and the negative injunction, "fear not, don't be scared" (*me phobou*).

Here is a paralysed man looking up to him from the pallet on which he had been carried to the feet of Jesus. "Take heart, my son," Jesus says (Matthew 9:2), and then, with that penetrating insight which saw the spiritual need behind the physical sickness, "your sins are forgiven." Hope is born. Healing of the whole person follows.

Here is a woman, plagued with haemorrhages and, probably, shunned by the people. Timidly, she touches the edge of his cloak. "Take heart, my daughter," Jesus says (Matthew 9:22): "your faith has healed you." Hope is born. A whole woman rejoins the community.

Here are three men, Peter, James and John, confronted with a spiritual reality in the transfiguration of Jesus the like of which they had never seen before. This is beyond their understanding, and they "fell on their faces in terror". "Stand up; do not be afraid," Jesus says (Matthew 17:7). He had said much the same – "Take heart! It is I; do not be afraid" (Matthew 14:27) – when he had come to them walking on the lake and they had thought it was a ghost. He was to say much the same when, after his resurrection, he came onto their path as they hurried from the tomb "in awe and great joy" – "Do not be afraid. Go and take word to my brothers . . ." (Matthew 28:10).

On their evangelistic mission they must have recalled the occasion of which Luke tells us (5:10) when, after the huge catch of fishes, Jesus had said to an awe-struck crew: "Do not be afraid; from now on you will be catching people."

The Gospels give us ample examples of incidents in which, though the actual words "cheer up" and "fear not" do not occur, hope came to the hopeless. I mention two:

(i) Luke (7:36ff.) describes brilliantly the meal in the Pharisee's house to which Jesus was invited and to which, uninvited, "a woman who was living an immoral life" also came. Unlike the host, secure in his respectability, the woman knows her need and pours out her devotion at the feet of Jesus. "Your faith has saved you; go in peace," says Jesus. You can leave the old order behind you – "your sins are forgiven". A new day is before you, a day of peace and wholeness, of integration with God and with society. Go in peace. There is hope ahead.

(ii) Luke alone of the evangelists gives us the picture of Zacchaeus, the superintendent of taxes who was very rich (19:1–10). Rich, but a despised member of society, "a sinner" who earned his living from the hated invader. But coming into contact with Jesus, the floodgates of his generosity are opened. The prospect of a new life dawns as he meets the Man of Hope. "Today salvation" – fulness of life – "has come to this house." The Son of Man has sought and saved the poor little rich man.

If *acts* such as these brought an infusion of hope to the men and women who came within the reach of Jesus, his whole *teaching* also shows him as the Man of Hope.

The sermon with which he opened his public ministry, in the Nazareth synagogue, was not simply the exposition of a passage from Isaiah. It was a nailing of his colours to the mast, an exposition of the purpose of his coming, a declaration of the heart of his messianic task. It was addressed to the underdog – "the poor, the prisoners, the blind, the broken victims" (Luke 4:16ff.) – no wonder that this passage is loved – and rightly – by the exponents, especially in Latin America, of liberation theology! Imagine the effect of this on a congregation of "unfortunates", of people hard hit politically and economically. Let us not so "over-spiritualize" the passage that we miss the force of its first impact. "All eyes in the synagogue were fixed on him . . . there was general approval; they were astonished that words of such grace should fall from his lips" (vv.20,22). It was a programme with hope at its heart.

But that was only a beginning. The Man of Hope gathered round him a little community of men and women – "not many wise . . . powerful or of noble birth" (as Paul was to say). "A little flock", that was how Jesus himself described them (Luke 12:32), liable to be scattered, with no great strength or cohesion of their own. But "have no fear, little flock; for your *Father* has chosen to give you the *kingdom*". We note that the Father is also King. The little flock belongs to him whose is the kingdom, the power and the glory. So the teaching of Jesus about "being of good courage" and of "not fearing" is not just whistling in the dark to keep our courage up. It is *based on the very nature of God*.

Jesus is the Man of Hope precisely because he knows God in this dual capacity. God is his Father – here is love. God is his King – here is authority. Jesus is in a relationship of both Son to a Father and Servant to a King. The Man of Hope is the Son-Servant, and from that relationship he derives at once his power and his serenity. From that relationship his little flock is to derive theirs – a power which is of a calibre totally unlike the power of the world, and a serenity which passes all understanding.

There is nothing facile about our Lord's repeated assurance on the folly of worry – ". . . I tell you not to be anxious about food and drink . . . and about clothes . . . Can anxious thought add a single day to your life? . . . Why be anxious about clothes? . . . Do not ask anxiously, 'What are we to eat? What are we to drink? What shall we wear?' . . . Do not be anxious about to-morrow" (Matthew 6:25,27,28,31,34). Even when the disciples are arrested and the authorities look most menacing, "do not worry about what you are to say" (10:19). And there is no need for Martha to fret and fuss in the kitchen (Luke 10:41). This teaching, I repeat, is not facile even though at first sight it might appear to be so. It springs from the fact that worry is the opposite of trust, of faith in the Father-King. Grasp that – or, rather, be grasped by it – and faith will be seen to be the under-girding reality of a life lived, as our Lord's was, as a son-servant of God. We can "hope and be unafraid".

So we see – as we have noted already and shall note again – that hope and faith are very close cousins. Indeed, hope can be described as faith looking forward.

There is a realism about this teaching which braces our muscles and strengthens our nerves. John in his Gospel (16:33) hears Jesus say to his "little flock": "In the world you will have suffering" – there is realism. But immediately he goes on: "But take heart! I have conquered the world" – there is *confidence* born of a hope which never envisages defeat. So Jesus' teaching ministry was always forward-looking, for hope is not concerned with what is past but with what is about to be; not with what men and women were but with what they may become; not with what has wrecked them but with what will make them in the days to come. Face to face with the woman caught in the act of adultery, Jesus does not minimize the sinfulness of the act – that is obvious enough to him and to her. But he does not linger over it. "Neither do I condemn you" – condemning is useless, unproductive. No: he is concerned with the woman's future life. "Go" – the very command is full of hope – "do not sin again". There is a new day ahead (John 8:11).

According to Mark (10:13–15), Jesus said: "Whoever does not accept the kingdom of God like a child will never enter it." What are the most characteristic marks of a child? Two, surely: trust and hope. *Trust* – in the sense of total dependence on the mother for nourishment and the father for support. In adult language, that is faith, the acknowledged need of grace, the acceptance of proffered aid. But *hope* also – in the sense in which we are defining it: expectancy.

A child has a minimum of life to look back on. He has everything to look forward to. So his capacity for anticipation is high; a thirst for the future which can hardly be satisfied. Watch the eyes of a child when he is promised a visit to the circus, the zoo, or whatever. Listen to him as he cries: "I can't wait!" Tell him about Christmas or the holidays, and he will count the days. Expectation – anticipation – the attitude of the tiptoe – *hope*. These are the marks of any normal child. "The kingdom of Heaven belongs to such as these." Unless we become like that there will be for us no entry into the meaning of God's reign. We shall always be looking back. We shall live the life of the stunted, the listless, the hope-less.

What surprises has God got in store for us up his ample sleeve? No wonder Cardinal Suenens is constantly teaching us about "the surprises of the Spirit"!

The Kingdom-theology which Jesus taught is big with hope. "The kingdom of Heaven is like a mustard seed . . . smaller than any other seed, *but* when it has grown it is taller than other plants . . ." (Matthew 13:31–32). It is "like yeast", a little insignificant-looking thing, but effervescent, full of life, able to make three measures of flour rise. It is, literally, *exciting* – the English word is derived from the Latin, and means to stimulate, set in motion, arouse. The "little flock" may be small, but they are the salt which keeps society from going bad (Matthew 5:13), the light which penetrates the darkness and which can never be mastered by it (Matthew 5:14, and cf: John 1:5).

The climax of the Kingdom-theology is presented in the picture of a heavenly banquet. The picture was a familiar one to the people of Jesus' time: Isaiah, for example, had spoken of a coming day when "on this mountain the Lord of Hosts will prepare a banquet of rich fare for all the peoples, a banquet of wines well matured . . ." (25:6). Similar language is used in the apocryphal writings. "One of the company" of those who were present at the Pharisee's dinner which Jesus attended said "happy are those who will sit at the feast in the kingdom of God" (Luke 14:15). Jesus himself spoke of a coming day when "from east and west, from north and south, people will come and take their places at the banquet in the kingdom of God" (Luke 13:29). He had told the people who were following him to expect some surprises on that day: "Many, I tell you, will come from east and west to sit with Abraham, Isaac, and Jacob at the banquet in the kingdom of Heaven. But those who were born to the kingdom will be thrown out into the dark . . ." (Matthew 8:11–12).

In all three synoptic recordings of the Last Supper the idea of a coming banquet is implicit in the words of the institution – Jesus will not again drink the fruit of the vine until the day when he drinks it new in the kingdom of his Father (Matthew 26:29; Mark 14:25; Luke 22:18). The supper round the table in Jerusalem was anticipatory. "It was a prior realization of the banquet of the Kingdom of God in advance of its universal fulfilment" (John V. Taylor: *Kingdom Come*, p.84). Every time the Eucharist is celebrated it looks forward in hope to the great consummation. It is "till he come". Wine speaks of joy and exuberance – everything in the

Kingdom will be new. The hallelujahs of heaven are anticipated in the here and now.

Richard Crashaw catches the feel of these Gospel records in his version of the hymn of St Thomas Aquinas:

> Come love! Come Lord! And that long day
> For which I languish, come away.
> When this dry soul those eyes shall see,
> And drink the unseal'd source of thee.
> When Glory's sun faith's shades shall chase,
> And for thy veil give me thy face.

Crashaw's poetic language is reflected more soberly in the Liturgy of Lima when the congregation prays as it celebrates the Eucharist:

Remember, Lord, all the servants of your church:
  bishops, presbyters, deacons,
  and all those to whom you have given gifts of
    ministry.
Remember also all our sisters and brothers
  who have died in the peace of Christ,
  and those whose faith is known to you alone:
  guide them to the joyful feast prepared
  for all peoples in your presence,
  with the blessed Virgin Mary,
  with the patriarchs and prophets, the apostles and
    martyrs . . .
  and all the saints for whom your friendship was life.
With all these we sing your praise
  and await the happiness of your kingdom

where with the whole creation,
finally delivered from sin and death,
we shall be enabled to glorify you
through Christ our Lord.

"In a variety of ways", John Macquarrie writes, "Christians participate in the dying and rising of Christ, and it is through their present experience of life in the body of Christ that they already have some understanding of the meaning of resurrection and eternal life" (*Christian Hope*, p.80). In the Eucharist, that "participation in the dying and rising of Christ" is focused and dramatized:

> Christ has died:
> Christ has risen:
> Christ will come again –

so the Christian congregation cries out at a focal point in the service. In that cry, its members not only look back to the historic moment of their Lord's death and resurrection, but they also in anticipation look forward to that End when he shall reign whose is the kingdom, the power and the glory. Standing, as it were, at midpoint between the first advent and the second, they renew their hope and revive their strength as they share in "those blest tokens of his passion".

The Christian's hope is exactly like the anchor . . . [it] bites the ocean-bed and enables us to ride fearless, however high the waves may dash.

C. F. D. Moule,
The Meaning of Hope, p. 27

3

Messages of Hope

The men who wrote the letters of the New Testament – Paul, the unknown writer of Hebrews, Peter, John, as well as the writer of the Revelation – were men of hope.

If we ask what was the basis of their hope, we shall have to say at least three things:

First, there were the writings of the Old Testament (and the apocryphal writings in so far as they were extant and available to them at that period). Those stalwart, rugged writers could have made their own the words of the seventeenth-century German hymn-writer: "All my hope on *God* is founded." God was the ground of their hope. That was the theme of chapter 1.

Secondly, there was the Christ-event, so recent, so vivid to their consciousness. The arrival and the impact of the Son of Man – his hope-full personality ("be of good cheer; don't be frightened"); his teaching about God and life; his vanquishing of death and sin; his resurrection and exaltation. If the Old Testament had held out to them a bud, the Christ-event showed them its flowering. Without the centrality of Christ to this astonishing development, there is no explanation of the phenomenon of the New Testament nor of the power of the Church's life and testimony down the centuries. New Testament hope rests firmly on the resurrection of Jesus Christ from the dead, and this is removed by a hemisphere from human optimism or sentimental cheerfulness. (On this contrast, see J. Macquarrie, *Christian Hope*, p.13).

Thirdly, there was the experience of those who were "the original eye-witnesses and servants of the gospel" (Luke 1:2). There were those two who went, terrified and hopeless, to the tomb expecting to find the dead body of their Lord. Their despondency turned to hope when the fact of the resurrection dawned on them. There were the two who set out, heavy-footed and heavy-hearted, from Jerusalem to their home eight long miles away at Emmaus. They were joined by the young risen Lord, who was known to them in the breaking of the bread in their own home (Luke 24:13ff.). There was the witness of many others to whom Jesus appeared – Paul spoke of "over five hundred of our brothers" (1 Corinthians 15:6).

The basis of the hope of the New Testament writers was firm. It is not as if any one of them sat down to write a thesis on hope. Not at all. Hope simply seeps through their writings with a kind of inevitability. It is so strong an aspect of their Christian life that every New Testament writer finds himself referring to it with the utmost naturalness.

We turn now to the evidence.

PAUL

In Romans 15:13, Paul refers to God as "the God of hope". The phrase does not occur again in the New

Testament. The *Revised English Bible* spells it out in what is something of a paraphrase: "God, who is the ground of hope". That may well be a correct rendering. Certainly it enshrines a profound truth. God is the base, the source, of the Christian's hope; the foundation, sure and unshakeable, on which the building of hope may be erected. Or, to change the metaphor, he is the source from which a fountain of hope may issue, springing up, entering into us, proceeding from us, providing, as Paul says in this passage, "all joy and peace as" we "lead the life of faith . . .". God is, in the words of the hymn, "the Lord of all hopefulness, Lord of all joy".

There is another way in which the phrase "the God of hope" can be interpreted. Just as "the King of love" means "the love-full King", so the God of hope may mean "the hope-full God", the God one of whose main characteristics is that he is always full of hope. He never despairs. Paul, in his hymn to love, says that love "hopes all things" (1 Corinthians 13:7). The *Revised English Bible* paraphrases: "there is no limit to . . . its hope"; J. B. Phillips: "love knows no fading of its hope". So here Paul would suggest that our God is one whose hope for his world, for his Church, for his humblest creature, never flags. His designs will never be defeated, his hopes never finally be thwarted. His patience is infinite.

It is hard for us creatures of a day to think in terms big enough to do justice to this aspect of God. The scientists, with their vision of the expanding universe, the slow evolution of life over countless millennia, may help us to escape from the shackles of a "God who is too small", and point us to one who "unresting, unhasting, and silent as light, nor wanting, nor wasting . . . ruleth in might". Perhaps a generation which has learned to think, with a touch of over-familiarity, of God as Father might learn to counter-balance that insight with the thought of a God of the galaxies and of the atoms – the hope-full God.

Even within the brief compass of human history, we can think of God as hopefully and patiently at work. His disappointments have been many. The owner of the vineyard spoken of in Isaiah's parable expected the vine "to yield choice grapes, but all it yielded was a crop of wild grapes" (5:2). If the world which the Creator saw to be good got spoiled by man's folly, then he would choose a people after his own heart. If that people failed him, then he would choose a godly remnant. If that remnant were reduced to twelve and one of those betrayed his Son, then he would use the eleven. If they all forsook that Son and fled, then God's patient purpose would be fulfilled by a Man on a cross, a Man resurrected, and, later, by a Spirit-filled Church.

The patient, hope-full God; John Henry Newman's *Gerontius* marvels at him:

> "In all his works most wonderful,
> Most sure in all his ways";

and then sings his own little *Gloria*:

> Glory to him who from the mire
> In patient length of days,
> Elaborated into life
> A people to his praise!

The infinite hope-full patience of God in the continuing creation of the universe, and in the preparation of a people for his service is reflected, as it were in miniature, in his re-creation of human beings. The material on which God has to work in the production of personalities "ordained to share the likeness of his Son" (Romans 8:29) proves recalcitrant – the clay proves obstinate in the hands of the Potter. But love never despairs. Hopefully, patiently, the heavenly Potter works on. Eventually something will appear which reflects his mind, and God will look on what he has made of that man or woman and say, as he did of the first creation: "It is good."

God, precisely because he is the hope-full God, seems to enjoy engaging in great experiments – whether the experiment has to do with a universe, or a Church, or a human personality. He is the God who is always making things new. That is why his people are a forward-looking people, renewed in hope at every Eucharist (see p. 45) till the day dawns when there shall be "new heavens and a new earth, in which justice will be established" (2 Peter 3:13).

So much for Paul's haunting phrase "the God of hope". (I have elaborated this in my *Paul: Portrait of a Revolutionary*, Hodder, 1984, pp.147ff. and 190–1.) Paul's theology is always closely related to life; his letters are directed to specific pastoral situations. Thus, in writing to the Corinthians, he had in mind an infant-church whose members were facing extreme difficulties. They were a minority group. They had problems ethical, sexual, theological. They had temptations to lose heart and give up the conflict. With this in mind, he sought to raise their sights. He pointed them to the resurrected Lord and their own future resurrection: "We know that he who raised the Lord Jesus to life will with Jesus raise us too, and bring us to his presence . . . No wonder we do not lose heart!" (2 Corinthians 4:14,16). So he launches out into a passage remarkable at once for its earthiness and for its outreach to the realms beyond death.

In 2 Corinthians, chapters 4 and 5, Paul sets out a series of contrasts:

The outward humanity in decay ....
...........................*inward renewal* (4:16)
Short-lived troubles ....*eternal glory* (4:17)
Things that are seen ....
...........................*things that are unseen* (4:18)
What is transient.................. *what is eternal* (4:18)
An earthly frame...
...........................*a building provided by God* (5:1)
A home in the body ....
...........................*a home with the Lord* (5:6–8)

Paul reaches the climax of his thesis at 5:10 with a mention of "the tribunal of Christ" where our lives are laid open, and each receives "what is due to him for his conduct in the body, good or bad". This idea of a "tribunal" (which occurs again in Romans 14:10) is no cause of terror for those in Christ, for through him they enjoy "peace with God" (Romans 5:1–2). But it adds a note of seriousness to living. There is a goal to be reached – and it could be missed. There can be no trivializing of life or of Christian discipleship when that is the end towards which we move.

There is in this passage a *realism* to Paul's view of life here and hereafter which is admirable. He does not seek to evade the evils which flesh is heir to. He looks troubles in the eye. He faces the reality of death – there is a demolition of the body ahead of everyone (5:1). There are groans (5:4) from which Christians are not exempt – just because a person is a Christian it does not mean that he treads a path strewn with roses; he is still part of a smitten creation. Does this mean that the apostle is a pessimist? By no means. He is a proximate realist and an ultimate optimist, because with a "confident expectancy" based on faith (5:7), he knows that death will be swallowed up in victory and Christ will ultimately reign. He defines his hope with a kind of monosyllabic simplicity – "we shall leave our home in the body and go to live with the Lord". That is all we need to know (not all we should like to know) about heaven, but it is enough to give meaning to our life here and to provide us with a lively expectation for the future. "Heaven is everlasting, for God is everlasting, and it is the fulfilment of man's meaning as created in the divine image and of God's infinite love for each and all. Thus heaven gives perspective to man's present existence, and man's life in this world is but a brief prelude to the goal for which he was created" (Michael Ramsey: *Sacred and Secular*, Longmans, 1965, p.3).

There is a destiny for which God has been shaping us (5:5). We are not here to drift – and then out into the dark. God is at work in us and co-operating with us in the making of characters who will live in his presence. For the fulfilment of that great co-operative enterprise and as a pledge of his being serious about it, he has given us the Spirit, source of life and power (5:5).

Further, he has given us an "*ambition*" (5:9), at once very simple and enormously demanding. It is to be "acceptable (well-pleasing) to him". To that goal every-thing is to be subjected. It will, as Paul says in Romans 12:1–2, call for a self-dedication to God which can best be defined as *worship*, worship of mind (so that our thinking processes are sharp and clear) and of heart (so that our love and affections are centred in and controlled by him). Thus we shall avoid being squeezed into the world's mould and shall find our liberty as sons and daughters of God. There is the tang of fresh air about such a dedication. There will, no doubt, be in such discipleship a reverence for tradition and for all that the past years have to teach us. But side by side with this there will be an openness to the new, an avoidance of the ruts, an element of the tiptoe. In short, a "confident expectancy". God is at work. Who knows where his next move will be?

The letter to the Ephesians is one of the great documents of the Christian Faith. Within it are two prayers (1:15–23 and 3:14–21), both of them deserving of the most careful study. For the purpose of this book, we turn to the first of the two.

It is a prayer, yet much more than a prayer. It begins with a thanksgiving and runs out into a great creedal affirmation, as if the writer had forgotten to end his prayer in any formal way and was carried up into adoration of the sovereign Christ, the One with all things put under his feet, the head of the Church which is his body.

The letter was an encyclical, a circular letter. In some early manuscripts the words "at Ephesus" (1:1) are missing. Presumably a gap was left in the text of the letter, and the church to which the circular came filled in its own name. So, before Paul launches out into his prayer (1:17), his mind turns towards a number of churches who would be receiving it and, probably, reading it at some gathering for worship. Some of these churches he had himself founded. Others he had visited in the course of his travels. In his mind's eye he can see a wide variety of people, his sisters and brothers in Christ, disciples of the one Lord, his and theirs. He knew their weaknesses, their sins, their foibles. But it is not of these that he thinks particularly now. Rather, he fastens on their "faith in the Lord Jesus and the love they bear towards all God's people" (1:15). Faith and love – that is all that matters, and for that he thanks God unceasingly (1:16). He *mentions* them before God – just the re-calling of a name or a face, thinking of them Godwards; that was enough.

What should he pray for them, these men and women, some of them persecuted for their faith, some of them despised for their allegiance to a crucified Jew? Should he pray for their physical safety? For provision for their material needs? For better organization of their little Christian communities and for better arrangements for their worship? All these would be good subjects for his prayer. But he passes them by. He will ask for one thing only – "the spiritual gifts of *wisdom* and *vision*, with the *knowledge* of him (Christ) that they bring". *Wisdom*

– which God imparts to those who love him. *Vision* –
unveiling of blind eyes, so that they are open to God's
disclosure of truth as and when he sees it right to act.
And *knowledge*, that experiential knowledge of Christ
which is so much more than intellectual furniture. It is
not that Paul despises the activities of the mind – far
from it; his was a mind always reaching out into the
immensities of truth. But he knew the limitations of
intellectual speculation and leaned heavily towards
expectant meditation on the truth of God. There is an
enlightenment which is not dependent on learning, as
Thomas Aquinas discovered while saying mass on the
morning of 6 December 1273: "I can do no more," he
declared; "such things have been revealed to me that all
I have written seems as straw, and I now await the end
of my life." The place of enlightenment for this great
scholar was the place of devotion, of response to revelation. So, in the words of Paul's prayer, his "inward
eyes" were "enlightened" (v.18), literally "the eyes of
the heart", that centre of the whole inner life, with its
thinking, feeling and volition. When a person loves God
with all his *heart*, his whole being goes out to him in
adoration and worship.

So Paul comes to the very core of his prayer for his
scattered friends. He prays *"that you may know what
is the hope to which he calls you"*. Here is our word,
hope, central to the whole prayer. Grasp that, and they
will find that it is like "an anchor for their lives, safe
and secure" (Hebrews 6:19). Grasp that, and they will
be able to celebrate "the truth that all the mystery of
our existence can find its meaning in the Word that was
made flesh, who shared our lives and our death, so that

in death we might live . . . Our existence is a gift of a loving God and, no matter how dark or however tragic it may be for us, it is never hopeless because God has come down into our darkness and death, and is risen again." (Gerard W. Hughes: *In Search of a Way*, Darton, Longman and Todd, 1986, p.122.) "There are no depths where he is not and . . . for the Christian nothing can ever be hopeless" (p.144).

"The hope to which he calls you" is filled out in the ensuing clauses, filled out in two closely packed sentences: (i) "how rich and glorious is the share he offers you among his people in their inheritance", and (ii) "how vast are the resources of his power open to us who have faith." Paul would say: "Look how rich you are: don't live as paupers. God has put in your hand a key to his bank: use it. God says to you as the father said to the elder brother in the parable: 'My boy, you are always with me, and everything I have is yours' " (Luke 15:31).

"Vast resources of divine power are available: don't live as weaklings." This is resurrection power, the same power that "raised Christ from the dead and enthroned him . . ." (v.20) above all conceivable powers in this age or in the age to come.

Such, then, is the prayer in chapter 1, a prayer with *hope* at its heart. With that hope pulsating in them, the Christians go to a world "without hope and without God" (2:12) and proffer the word of life. The "one hope held out in God's call to them" (4:4) they share, for the hope is a Person, even "Christ Jesus our hope" (1 Timothy 1:1). (I have dealt more fully with this passage in my *The Prayers of the New Testament*, Mowbray, reprint edition, 1984, pp.126ff.)

The letter to the Colossians has much in common with Ephesians. It takes a little further the subject of hope – in three references, all in the first chapter.

(i) In vv.3 and 4, the writer thanks God for his readers' faith and love, as he had done in Ephesians 1:15. Here he sees these two basic qualities as springing from hope. Were it not for hope, faith and love would be absent or, at least, enfeebled. But the point of interest in v.5 is that the writer speaks of hope as having been *stored up in heaven* for the readers, and as having been learned of only when the message of the true Gospel came to them. Prior to the Christ-event (of which we spoke earlier, pp.38) the hope of the prophets and the psalmists had about it a strong element of anticipation of an event yet future. After the Christ-event, there was a sense of fulfilment of hope hitherto not experienced. Of course, the future hope of the Christians was still anticipatory – there was an End to history, a consummation of revelation, to which they still looked forward. But that hope was based on the rock of Christ's incarnation, passion and resurrection, and so was of a quality of which the Old Testament knew little. With his coming, a new day had dawned, and hope took on a new dimension.

(ii) In v.23, there is a note of warning made the more solemn by the picture of the world to which, before their conversion, the readers of the letter had belonged. They had been "alienated from God, his enemies in heart and mind" (v.21). But now they have been reconciled, brought into God's presence to be holy and without blame or blemish. There must be no retrogression, no moving from their foundations, *no dislodgement from the hope* offered in the Gospel and accepted by them when first they knew the Lord.

The pictures given in these words are vivid; they speak for themselves, and call for no comment but only for heeding.

(iii) In v.27, the text is difficult. The writer is referring to the revelation of what we have called the Christ-event, hidden hitherto but now disclosed to God's people. The *Revised English Bible* translates: "To them [i.e., to God's people] he chose to make known what a wealth of glory is offered to the Gentiles in this secret purpose: Christ in you, the hope of glory."

When Paul wrote of us all being "deprived of the divine glory" (Romans 3:23), he meant that the divine image in which we were created has been marred and distorted by sin. But now, by God's intervention, a new process has been set in motion by which the old image will be restored. This is the "hope of glory", entirely Christ-centred – "Christ in you, the hope of glory".

The *New English Bible* rendering "the hope of the glory *to come*", makes the concept too exclusively future. The text reads simply "the hope of glory". That process of glorification begins here and now. True, it will reach its consummation only in a future life. But –

> if thus, good Lord, thy grace be given
> our glory meets us *ere* we die;
> *before* we upward pass to heaven
> we taste our immortality.

The glorifying presence of Christ in us must not be futurized. He abides in us and we abide in him *on the road* to heaven. Meanwhile, on the road, "we exult in the hope of the divine glory that is to be ours", a hope which "is no phantasy" (Romans 5:2,5).

This must be added: in this verse (1:27) "in you" can equally well be translated "among you". Paul is writing about the Church, Christ's body, the Church of which Paul became a servant (vv.24–25), God's people (v.26) to whom he chose to make his wealth of glory known. "Christ among you", saving, sanctifying, reaching out through an entity which reflects his very being, *there* in that body corporate is the hope of glory. "In you", "among you"; there is no contradiction here, only complementarity.

In the Pastoral Epistles (1 and 2 Timothy and Titus), the word "hope" occurs only four times:

In 1 Timothy 1:1, the writer, in a remarkable phrase, uses it almost as a title of his Lord – "Jesus Christ our hope". Here in a nutshell is all that we have been saying about the Christ-event as the main basis of the New Testament doctrine of hope. Jesus Christ is the source, the foundation, the very essence of our confidence.

(It is noteworthy that Jeremiah (14:8) had addressed God as "Hope of Israel". John Macquarrie comments: ". . . for Israel God and hope stand in the closest association – indeed, they are almost identified" (*Christian Hope*, p.31). The writer of 1 Timothy had an Old Testament analogy on which to work.)

In Titus 1:2 the "hope of eternal life" is descriptive of "the truth enshrined in our religion". We have to wait until 2:13 to find that hope elaborated. Clearly the writer is looking to the great consummation of all things, the End towards which history is moving "when the splendour of our great God and Saviour Christ Jesus will appear". It was the purpose of God that we should "in hope become heirs to eternal life", "justified" as we are "by his grace" (3:7). That is a present reality, but it awaits its fulfilment at the great Day. The hope of that day when eternity will again intersect with time and "the splendour of our great God and Saviour Jesus Christ will appear" gives thrust to the Pauline Gospel. Omit that apocalyptic element and the Pauline message is robbed of its virility.

PETER

The first letter of Peter can reliably be dated about AD 63 or 64. That date speaks volumes. For Nero was on the throne, and that augured ill for the little Christian communities listed in the opening verse of the letter. How vividly Peter describes them! – "the scattered people of God living as aliens in Pontus, Galatia, Cappodocia, Asia, and Bithynia" (was this a list of the places Peter had visited on his missionary work en route to Rome?). "Scattered . . . living as aliens" – it does not sound very comfortable or secure; they were conscious that here, in this world, they had no continuing city but that they were simply passing through on the road to that "city with firm foundations, whose architect and builder is God". "Living as aliens" in a society which understood neither them nor the faith which they professed; who was this Jesus, this crucified Messiah, on whom their hope so obviously depended? "Aliens" – and therefore liable to be accused of disloyalty to the authorities, themselves having "a rival king, Jesus" (Acts 17:7). "Aliens" – and so likely to be pounced upon for persecution, if the local games called for victims to be hauled out into the arena for ignominy or sport. It is not easy to live out your faith if you are members of a tiny minority movement and if you bear in your body the marks which make you recognizable as being a follower of the Lord Jesus.

So it is that there is much in this letter which speaks of suffering or at least hints at it; and much that speaks of Christ's suffering even unto death. The readers of the letter have had "to suffer trials of many kinds" – fiery trials which test them (1:6–7). Had not the spirit of Christ in the old prophets pointed forward to suffering (1:11)? As "aliens in a foreign land", they find themselves maligned "as wrongdoers" (2:11–12). Sometimes they are the victims of "ignorance and stupidity" (2:15). The servants among them will sometimes find that their masters are unjust, and will have to endure "the pain of undeserved suffering" (2:18–19). When that is the case, they are to remember the servant Christ who himself suffered . . . and left an example that they should follow in his steps (2:21ff.). They may find themselves wronged and abused (3:9); they may suffer for doing right (3:14). They will have to make their defence when challenged (3:15 – is there a suggestion here of a case in the law courts?); their Christian conduct may be maligned and if so that will involve suffering (3:16–17). They may have to undergo physical suffering, as Christ did (4:1); they will be misunderstood (4:4). All this is indeed a "fiery ordeal" but to be "reviled" and to "suffer" is to share in the suffering of Christ and to confess his name to the glory of God. "Their Maker will not fail them" (4:12–19). And, "after your brief suffering, the God of all grace . . . will himself restore, establish, and strengthen you . . ." (5:10).

Yes: the background of this letter is one of testing and of suffering – that is clear. Those who have had dealings with their fellow-Christians in Uganda who suffered under Idi Amin or Milton Obote or those who have felt the heavy pressure of apartheid in South Africa are in a position to appreciate the situation reflected in this letter. But there is no hint of self-pity in these chapters; no sense of an inferiority complex on the part of the Christians. On the contrary, there is a sense of resilience, of *making* something out of the stresses, of pure gold coming out of the furnace. What is the secret? It is found in one word – *hope*.

That note is struck at the beginning of the letter. The greeting over (1:1–2), Peter breaks out into a doxology – "praised be the God and Father of our Lord Jesus Christ!" Before he touches on the difficulties and complexities of discipleship in those little communities, he lifts up his heart in praise to *God* and "his great mercy". That is the best cordial, if there are any drooping spirits among his readers – God and his mercy! Then he spells out the reason for his thanksgiving – God has given him and his readers "new birth into a living hope". What a vivid phrase! "New birth" – out of the confines of the old womb of their pre-Christian experience, into an entirely new sphere. They can breathe. They can look out, and forward, and up. They have a living hope, a "confident expectancy". How has this come about? Peter is in no doubt – "*by the resurrection* of Jesus Christ from the dead" this birth into a living hope has taken place. As we wrote earlier: "New Testament hope rests firmly on the resurrection of Jesus Christ from the dead, and is thus removed by a hemisphere from human optimism or sentimental cheerfulness" (see pp. 49–50). It is unique, in that it springs from a unique event.

Then, in a delightful phrase, Peter speaks of this resurrection hope as being "of an inheritance, reserved in heaven for you", totally safe in God's keeping, totally impervious to any kind of attrition (v.4). It is within them, and it is waiting for them – in all its rich fulfilment.

No wonder, then, that Peter begins his letter with a doxology! Lest any of his readers had missed the point, the central point, he comes back to it in v.21 of his first chapter: The faith and hope of the members of these churches are not in themselves, or in a new form of religion or a new philosophy, but they are fixed on God, the "God who raised [Christ] from the dead and gave him glory". Theirs is a resurrection hope; and that is indefeasible.

> All my hope on God is founded;
> he doth still my trust renew.

It may be that, when Peter came to write (in 3:13ff.) of his readers making their defence "when anyone challenges you to justify the hope which is in you", he had in mind a public law-court scene. Some of their members had been arrested for alleged disloyalty to the Emperor or his representative, and they were arraigned and had to answer the charges. He hints that the situation is enough to scare them, but he exhorts: "Have no fear of other people; do not be perturbed." But the passage is capable of a much wider interpretation. Their ordinary social and business life would present them with plenty of situations in which a challenge would be made to them about the hope that was in them. Such a challenge was in fact an opportunity, and it should be seized as such. Their hope is not to be hugged within them. It is to be shared.

Sometimes it will best be shared with *nothing* being said. The Christian's life will be more vocal than his words. In the opening verses of chapter 3, Peter envisages a situation where a Christian wife is married to an unbelieving husband. He will likely "be won over *without a word being said*", when he sees the beauty of his wife's constant behaviour. (In modern literature, Dostoevsky gives a classic illustration of such a happening in Sonia's wordless love breaking down the barriers and bringing resurrection-life to Raskolnikov – at the end of *Crime and Punishment*.)

But time and time again there will be occasions when a word *may* be spoken – and should. There might conceivably be a public debate. Far more frequently, there will be a challenge or a wistful question to be answered – in a casual meeting with a friend, on a walk, over a drink. Such opportunities should not be wasted – nor will they be if "the hope within them" is there like a heartbeat steadily pulsating, animating them.

But *how* is the case to be made? Are there conditions to its efficacy? Yes, indeed:

(i) "Hold Christ in your hearts in reverence as Lord" (3:15). You do not represent a party. You do not "hold a position". You revere your Lord and owe him undivided allegiance. No doubt as to whose you are and whom you serve!

(ii) "Be *ready* to make your defence." You are prepared to be "a fool for Christ's sake", if need be. But it is not helpful to be more foolish than you need be! Let your questioner see that your belief has substance to it. "I think: I believe: I am convinced" will carry more weight than an oft-repeated "I feel". Have your defence ready.

(iii) "Keep your conscience clear" (3:16). No compromises with evil!

Given these things, the Christian can make his case with quiet confidence. But even so, it must be done "with courtesy and respect" (3:15). The first word "courtesy" is used by Paul as one of the marks of the character of *Jesus* (2 Corinthians 10:1; translated as "gentleness" in the *Revised English Bible*). The second word is used of reverence toward God or respect for one's fellows. Combine these two words and you have an outline of the ideal approach of a Christian to one who is enquiring about the Christian hope. It is an approach of respect for the other person's personality, of reverence for him or her as a human being. There is no harsh thrusting of the truth down his throat; no attempt at intellectual or spiritual rape. This is not proselytizing on which you are engaged: it is evangelism.

And evangelism is the offering of something (some One) infinitely dear to you to a brother or sister with whom you want the privilege of sharing your treasure. There is a world of difference between proselytizing and evangelizing when this latter word, so central to the New Testament, is rightly understood.

At the back of Peter's mind, as he writes to these "scattered people of God now living as aliens" and colouring all he had to say to them in their suffering under persecution, was the figure of Christ himself. Peter was thinking of him, surely, when he wrote: "Do not repay wrong with wrong, or abuse with abuse; on the contrary, respond with blessing..." (3:9). He knew, and many of his readers knew, the passage in Isaiah about the suffering Servant of God, who "was maltreated, yet he was submissive and did not open his mouth" (53:7). He was thinking of Christ when he wrote: "It is better to suffer for doing right ... than for doing wrong", and he goes on directly: "Christ ... suffered for our sins (an alternative reading has 'died for our sins') once for all, ... that he might bring us to God" (3:17–18) and, later, he writes starkly: "Christ endured bodily suffering" (4:1). The towering figure of the suffering and resurrected Christ is behind all he writes and he is the source also of his readers' hope and endurance.

HEBREWS

The letter to the Hebrews, though very different from the first letter of Peter, has this in common with it: it is written to Christians for whom the going has been hard. The letter, if such it can be called, is addressed to people whose danger is that they might regress rather than progress, that they might slip back, or even fall away: "See to it ... that no one among you has the wicked and faithless heart of a deserter from the living God" (3:12); "What we must fear ... is that ... any one of you should be found to have missed his opportunity" (4:1); "Do not ... throw away your confidence, for it carries a great reward" (10:35). There is a danger, too, of a continuing immaturity, an indication that the readers were content to keep on "discussing the rudiments of Christianity", the elementary things, instead of "advancing towards maturity" (6:1–2).

If the trials of the readers of 1 Peter come mostly from without, the dangers of those to whom Hebrews is sent come largely from within (though the reference in 12:4 may well speak of persecution from pagan opponents – "you have not yet resisted to the point of shedding your blood").

The constant theme – it runs through the letter – is to "hold fast to the faith ..." (4:14); not to "throw away your confidence" but to endure and "win what [God] has promised" (10:35–36); they must "run with resolution the race which lies ahead of" them (12:1); they must brace their "drooping arms and shaking knees" (12:12); they must bear "the stigma that [Jesus] bore" (13:13).

The writer, in concluding this letter, calls it "my appeal" (13:22). It is that. It is full of warnings and exhortations and imperatives. But such things, by themselves, could amount to little more than beating a dead horse. There is no good news in an order, or in an appeal, or in an exhortation. In truth, Hebrews is far more than this. For it is an epistle of *hope*. And that hope is centred in Christ.

The writer bids us look to him: "because he himself has passed through the test of suffering, he is able to help those who are in the midst of their test" (2:18). "Jesus the Son of God" is their great high priest – "one who has been tested in every way as we are, only without sinning". To him they can come and "receive mercy and find grace to give us timely help" (4:14–16). Then there are those who have gone before them, people like Abraham, who "give powerful encouragement to us, who have laid claim to his protection by grasping the hope before us. *We have that hope as an anchor for our lives . . .*" (6:18–19). This is more than exhortation. This is spiritual reality centred in Christ. An anchor is that which keeps a boat from disaster when the storm is raging; its flukes bite the ocean-bed and enable the ship to ride fearless, however furious the surface-water may be.

When we come to chapter 11, we find faith and hope in close juxtaposition (v.1). (We are reminded of our definition of hope as *confident* expectancy.) The writer summons up the heroes of the Old Testament, a mixed body of frail mortals like ourselves but all of them, in some sense, people of faith. "By faith, by faith, by faith" – so the refrain runs. But what does he mean by faith? It is very close to the central subject of this study, *hope*. If hope is faith looking forward, faith on tiptoe, then Abraham was a good example of it, "for he was looking forward to a city with firm foundations, whose architect and builder is God" (v.10). If Moses was resolute in determining to leave the luxuries of Egypt for the perils and privations of his desert-mission, his resolution was that of a man "who saw the invisible God" (v.27). That is faith looking upward and forward. That is hope.

I am writing this on All Saints' Day. One's mind has been full of "this great cloud of witnesses around us" (12:1), not only those people of faith and hope of whom the author of Hebrews writes at such length and with such power, but also those who lived in the days of the incarnate Christ and called him, with a wonderful simplicity, "our hope" (1 Timothy 1:1). Then one has thought of that great company, whom no man can number, who have never seen Christ in the flesh, yet "who love him; and trusting in him now without seeing him ... are filled with a glorious joy too great for words" (1 Peter 1:8). These have been – and are – men and women of hope, who "run with resolution the race which lies ahead of" them, precisely because their "eyes are fixed on Jesus, the pioneer and perfecter of faith" (Hebrews 12:1,2). They are men and women of hope. They can feel the tug of the anchor, and they know that all is well. Their hope is set on Christ.

FIRST LETTER OF JOHN

It may be a cause for surprise that, when we come to the *Johannine writings* (Gospel and Epistles), *with one exception* the noun "hope" does not occur at all. The verb "hope" occurs in the Gospel once, and that in a context which has no bearing on our theme – "Moses on whom you have set your hope" (5:45). The verb "hope" occurs twice in the Johannine Epistles, and that in contexts which are purely personal and local – "I hope to visit you" (2 John:12) and "I hope to see you very soon" (3 John:14). That is all.

To the exception, then, we turn, for it occurs in a passage of great importance – "every man that hath this hope in him purifieth himself, even as he is pure" (1 John 3:3). So runs the Authorized Version. We must look at the translation more carefully in a moment. But, first, the context.

In the *Revised English Bible*, chapter 3 is given the heading: "How Christians live together." Clearly, it is in a state of continual surprise and wonderment! – wonderment at their present status and astonishment at what awaits them.

If tradition is right, this letter was written by the apostle John in his extreme old age. Certainly there is a repetitiveness about it which might well be that of a man advanced in years and in discipleship, who was looking back over the way that God had led him and recalling what he had seen of the grace of God at work in himself and in his fellow-Christians. The miracle of God's grace in granting them the status of his own "children" had never gone stale on him. "That is what we are", he says in a tone of astonishment (v.1), and, lest we should miss the point, he repeats it in v.2 – "we are now God's children". *Now*; we do not have to wait for our sonship to be a reality. All we have to do is to recognize it, to rejoice in it, to explore it, and to live in the power of it. (In an aside at the end of v.1, John expresses no surprise that this momentous fact does not register with "the world". As Paul put it: "the world failed to find him by its wisdom" (1 Corinthians 1:21). The Father has family secrets for his children.)

There is a confident assurance about this assertion which is the birthright of the people of God. It gives them a foothold when all the world is floundering. They have a Father, with all that that entails by way of rights of access for the children; all that he has is theirs.

The note of positive assertion is followed – but only briefly – by one of agnosticism. It is a healthy note. Over large tracts of life and experience and of the future we have to write: "We do not know. There has been no disclosure." Perhaps it is a mark of maturity to grant our ignorance – cocksureness is a mark of youth and should not too often intrude into middle or old age. "What we shall be has not yet been disclosed" (v.2). We live in the world of "not yet", the interim-period between the "now" of our physical existence on this planet and the "then" of the world to come, the "here" of this world and the "there" of the beyond. We know very little of the lineaments of that life and we might as well admit it.

"BUT we know...". Back comes the old letter-writer to the positive assertions of faith – "we know that when Christ appears we shall be like him, because we shall see him as he is." There is an End to history. So there is a climax to life – we do not lurch through the world and then out into the dark. Any Christian scheme of things which has no eschatology (no doctrine of the Last Things, or, perhaps better, no doctrine of the Coming One) is a poor maimed thing (see the notes on Titus 2:13, p.63).

"We shall be like him, because we shall see him as he

is." Does not that bunch of monosyllables tell us much? It tells us something – everything we *need* to know. This is the End, in the sense of the goal, the climax, the apogee, the culmination of our strivings. Here throughout our life we have seen "only puzzling reflections in a mirror" but then "we shall see face to face" (1 Corinthians 13:12). Here there have been doubtings and darkness and temptation to abandon the struggle and to desert. Here, worst of all, we have, so often and so desperately, been *un*like him. There "we shall be like him, because we shall see him as he is." Here the transfiguration of our personalities has been so slow and subject to so many setbacks. There, there will be growth unhindered.

It is this hope to which John refers in v.3 – the confident expectation that this person, maimed by sin, his own and that of others, marked with all the weaknesses of temporality, will be like him. Made in the image of God and marred by the sin of the world, the image of God will be restored and God will be able to say of the new creation as he did of the old: "it is good", and of his work "*consummatum est*".

"He who has this hope" – who has grasped it and made it his own; who indeed has been grasped by it; who has this hope within him like a pulsating heart – this person finds within him a power other than his own. "He purifies himself"; "makes himself pure" (*Revised English Bible*). The translation *could* smack of self-effort, but it is difficult to improve on it. Nevertheless, I believe that self-effort is far from the mind of the writer. The hope itself does its purifying work. John would say: "let this hope operate within you and, without your noticing it, the purifying process will begin and go on. You do not consciously think about the beating of your heart; you are not for ever taking your pulse; but the pulsating work of that wonderful machine goes on day and night. Let the fact of your divine sonship and the hope, the confident expectancy of your being 'like him', be the pulsating power of your continuing development."

A discipline is implied in the fulfilment of this hope. At that meeting with the Master when we see him face to face, we want to hear him say: "Well done!", and that entails the hard slog, the thorny path of those who take up the cross to follow him.

There is one other aspect of the power of hope which should not go unmentioned. We have been looking at it as a purifying agency in the Christian disciple. But it is effective in a direction other than the disciple's own life. It will affect his attitude to others. Paul has a pregnant phrase in his hymn to love in 1 Corinthians 13 – in v.7 he says that "love . . . *hopeth* all things", or, as the *Revised English Bible* puts it, "there is no limit to its . . . *hope*". By this we may take it that Paul means that, when the love of God is shed abroad in us, our approach to others is radically altered. One of its effects will be that we have hope even for the most unlovable. If God has been able to shed abroad his love in *my* heart, may I not then assume that nobody is hopeless?

THE REVELATION OF JOHN

The Revelation of John is essentially a pastoral letter. It is written to encourage small Christian communities to stand firm under persecution.

The word "hope" (noun and verb) does not occur in the book. That is not to say that the book has nothing to contribute to the subject. Far from it. Indeed, the opening chapter, which is autobiographical, sets the tone of the whole book. It is the story of a man whose hope, almost extinguished, was kindled into flame. Look at him:

It was Sunday morning, and he was far from home. He felt very keenly the separation from his friends and the lack of common worship which had been part of the pattern of his life when he lived on the mainland. Now he was an exile living on a little island which was the base for a prison-camp. The sea spoke to him, not of beauty but of the long distance which yawned between him and his friends in Christ.

No wonder John was depressed! He was there precisely because he had been faithful to his Lord – "because I had preached God's word and borne my testimony to Jesus" (1:9). Was that all the reward he got – separation, deportation and a job working in the mines? During his banishment, his depression was worst on Sunday mornings, for at home on the mainland the little Eucharist service in his house or in the house of one of his friends had meant almost everything to him. Had God forsaken him?

Then God touched him. John heard a voice. He turned – to see a figure radiant and glorious. He fell at his feet as though dead. But he felt the touch of a strong hand and he heard a voice: "Do not be afraid; I am the first and the last, and I am the living One; I was dead and now I am alive for evermore, and I hold the keys of death and Hades." If *that* was true, then John could face the future with security and *hope*.

The letters to the seven churches (chapters 2 and 3) are addressed to churches which were outposts of the Kingdom in an alien environment. Each letter begins with a description of the Lord of the Church – "the One who holds the seven stars in his right hand"; "the First and the Last, who was dead and came to life again", and so on. These descriptions themselves must have brought hope to the readers of the letters. They found themselves summoned to look *up* to God before they looked *out* at the dangers posed by a pagan world, or *in* to the frailties of their own discipleship. Rebukes there certainly are. But there is much encouragement and always that pointing forward to the Day when faithfulness will be rewarded, when "in the presence of my Father and his angels I shall acknowledge him as mine" (3:5); to that vision of the "new Jerusalem which is coming down out of heaven from my God" (3:12); to that "place beside me on my throne" (3:21). These are genuine messages of hope to beleaguered communities in Asia Minor.

The chapters which follow the letters to the seven churches are, in part, pretty terrifying. The language which is employed is graphic, highly-coloured, and largely *cypher* language. These are tracts for bad times; and such tracts must be written in language which the persecuted can understand and the persecutor cannot. It is the kind of thing which, in pre-Gorbachev days, the underground Christian Church in Russia propagated and called *samizdat* – dissident literature privately distributed. (Thus, Nero is not openly referred to: he is 666; Rome is called Babylon. . . .)

These chapters reflect a realistic assessment of the universal sinfulness of mankind and the inevitability of divine judgement. "Down below", wrote the historian Herbert Butterfield, "there slumbers all the time the volcano that lies in human nature, and an unexpected cataclysm may bring it into activity" (*Christianity and History*, p.31). But down in the heart of Christianity, and not least in the prayers of this vivid apocalyptic book, there is ground for what Bishop Charles Gore used to call an "ultimate optimism". How can this be so? Because the writer of the Revelation bases his philosophy of history (if we may call it that) on a fundamental doctrine of resurrection. "I was dead and now I am alive for evermore, and I hold the keys of death and Hades." That is how the book begins (1:18). "I am coming soon, and bringing with me my recompense to repay everyone according to what he has done! I am the Alpha and the Omega . . ." (22:12,13). That is how the book ends. It reaches its climax with the ringing of the bell of the eschatological hope: " 'Come!' say the Spirit and the bride. 'Come!' let each hearer reply . . . He who gives this testimony says: 'Yes, I am coming soon!' Amen. Come, Lord Jesus!" (22:17,20).

The writer of the Revelation will have no truck with the kind of God presented in certain American pulpits in the years between the First and the Second World Wars and parodied by Richard Niebuhr: "A God without wrath brought men without sin into a kingdom without judgement through the ministrations of a Christ without a cross" (*The Kingdom of God in America*, 1937, p.193). On the contrary, here in this book is a God of power and majesty, at work in judging and saving activity who will not rest until the vision of the new Jerusalem, the Holy City coming down out of heaven from God, is realized. There, for him, is the hope which must be fulfilled, for it is based on the very character of God himself and on his demonstration of that character in the resurrection of his Son.

Given this God and given this hope, the members of those little churches may *sing*. The book is studded with a series of ejaculations of worship and praise – "splendid Christian enthronement psalms", as C.F.D. Moule has described them (*The Birth of the New Testament*, p.23). They can be found in 4:8,11; 5:9–10,12,13; 7:10,12; 11:15,17–18; 15:3–4; 19:1–8; 22:20.

COMMENT

Hope – "the space where miracles happen".

Mother Teresa

4

Hope *versus* Despair

The young Church, as it embarked on its missionary course, was a community of hope. In one sense, that hope was a hope already *fulfilled*. It is interesting that in the Acts of the Apostles, apart from two instances where the word "hope" is used in a purely "secular" sense (the hope of profit, Acts 16:19, and the hope of coming safely through the storm, 27:20), "hope" is always used in the context of the resurrection of the dead (2:26; 23:6; 24:15; 26:6,7; 28:20). The hope that there would be a resurrection of good and bad was part and parcel of Pharisaic belief (chapter 1, p.34). In the resurrection of Jesus from the dead Paul saw a fulfilment of that hope in which, as a Pharisee, he had been brought up. Christ was the first-fruits (1 Corinthians 15:20). The resurrection hope had been vindicated on the first Easter morning.

But in another sense, the hope of the young Church was a hope fixed on the future. Its members had a lively hope that, in the very near future, their Lord would return. The delay of the fulfilment of that hope was a cause of difficulty to many of them, and Paul had to do some teaching work on this point. Some thought the day was "already here" (2 Thessalonians 2:2); some were concerned about "dates and times" (1 Thessalonians 5:1); others were puzzled about the state of those Christians who had already died without seeing the coming of the Lord (1 Thessalonians 4:13). The Church survived its disappointment of an early return, and went to the world with a hope the stronger for its immediate disappointment.

To the hope of a Day when the secrets of men's hearts would be revealed, an "assize" when wrongs would be righted, the Church held fast, though no doubt there were many differences in the way that Day was envisaged. But the hope of the Church was not dependent on the "how" or the "when" of the Coming. The early Christians had a burning inner conviction that the prayer Jesus had taught them – "thy Kingdom come" – would indeed be fulfilled. They were the "interim people", committed to the eucharistic life "till he come", empowered by the Spirit for the task of world-wide evangelization. So the little communities sprang up, each new-born member a witness to the power of the hope, each day a new opportunity to enter into the confident expectancy that the Day would surely come when "he would reign".

One of the things which astonished the pagan world was the strength of the hope manifested by the early Christians. No persecution could quench it. Indeed, the more fierce the persecution, the more purely did the flame of hope burn. The rabble might produce false witnesses and the Council arraign Stephen, but the man with the face "like the face of an angel" (Acts 6:15) died, after his stoning, a literally Christ-like death (7:59–60), upheld by a never-dying hope. "The blood of the martyrs was the seed of the Church" – Tertullian was right.

The hope was unquenchable and it has continued all down the centuries of the Church's life. Look at half-a-dozen examples; they could easily be multiplied many times:

Cyprian, Bishop of Carthage (d. 258), wrote to a man by the name of Donatus: "This seems a cheerful world, Donatus, when I view it from this fair garden, under the shadow of these vines. But if I climbed some great mountain and looked out over the wide lands, you know very well what I would see. Brigands on the high road, pirates on the seas, in the amphitheatres men murdered to please the applauding crowds, under all roofs misery and selfishness. It is a really bad world, Donatus, an incredibly bad world. Yet in the midst of it I have found a quiet and holy people. They have discovered a joy which is a thousand times better than any pleasures of this sinful life. They are despised and persecuted, but they care not. They have overcome the world. These people, Donatus, are the Christians . . . and I am one of them." *There* is the power of hope.

Chrysostom, Bishop of Constantinople (d. 407), wrote: "The waves have risen and severe storms are upon us, but we do not fear drowning, for we stand firmly upon a rock. Let the sea rage, it cannot break the rock. Let the waves rise, they cannot sink the boat of Jesus. What are we to fear? Death? 'Life to me means Christ, and death is gain.' Exile? 'The earth and its fullness belong to the Lord.' The confiscation of our goods? 'We brought nothing into this world, and we shall surely take nothing from it.' I have only contempt for the world's threats, I find its blessings laughable. I have no fear of poverty, no desire for wealth. I am not afraid of death nor do I long to live, except for your good. Do you not hear the Lord saying: 'Where two or three are gathered in my name, there am I in their midst'? Will he be absent, then, when so many people united in love are gathered together? Let the world be in upheaval. I hold to his promise and read his message; that is my protecting wall and garrison. What message? 'Know that I am with you always, until the end of the world!' " *There* is the power of hope.

Dunstan, Archbishop of Canterbury (d. 988), was described by one of his students as being "oak-like in hope". This is what sustained him through the calumnies which were his lot. After his death, when the oak had had time to grow, his work was seen to be of quality, and people turned to the Church to find in it a source of light in a darkling world. *There* is the power of hope.

Thomas More (d. 1535) wrote to his daughter Margaret from prison before his martyrdom: "I cannot . . . mistrust the grace of God. I will not mistrust him, Meg, though I shall feel myself weakening and on the verge of being overcome with fear. I shall remember how St Peter at a blast of wind began to sink because of his lack of faith, and I shall do as he did; call upon Christ and pray to him for help. And then I trust he shall place his holy hand on me and in the stormy seas hold me up from drowning. And finally, Margaret, I know this well: that without my fault he will not let me be lost. I shall, therefore, with good hope commit myself wholly to him. And if he permits me to perish for my faults, then

I shall serve as praise for his justice. But in good faith, Meg, I trust that his tender pity shall keep my poor soul safe and make me commend his mercy . . . Nothing can come but what God wills. And I am very sure that, whatever that be, however bad it may seem, it shall indeed be the best." *There* is the power of hope.

John Bunyan (d. 1688) put his hope into the mouth of Mr Standfast in the *Pilgrim's Progress*: "This river has been a terror to many . . . but now methinks I stand easy . . . The thought of what I am going to, and of the conduct that awaits me on the other side, doth lie as a glowing coal at my heart." *There* is the power of hope.

Dietrich Bonhoeffer (d. 1945), immediately before the summons which led to his death ("Prisoner Bonhoeffer, take your things and come with us"), gave his companions an exposition of Isaiah 53:5 ("through his stripes we are healed") and of 1 Peter 1:3 ("Blessed be the God and Father of our Lord Jesus Christ, which according to his abundant mercy hath begotten us again into a lively hope by the resurrection of Jesus Christ from the dead"). Then came his message to his trusted English friend, Bishop George Bell: "Tell him that for me this is the end, but also the beginning." *There* is the power of hope.

Hope runs like a golden thread through the history of the Church, linking the generations. It is one of the distinguishing signs which mark out the community of hope from the dark world in which that community is set. Here is a contrast worth noting.

God of Hope

In one of his *Parochial and Plain Sermons*, J. H. Newman wrote:

> We are in a world of mystery, with one bright *Light* before us, sufficient for our proceeding forward through all difficulties. Take away this *Light* and we are utterly wretched – we know not where we are, how we are sustained, what will become of us and of all that is dear to us, what we are to believe, and why we are in being. But with it we have all and abound.*

It would be hard to find better words in which to draw the contrast between the person who has the Christian hope and him who has it not. The point is made the clearer if, in the quotation, we substitute the word *hope* for the word *Light* in the two places where the latter word occurs. Reader, please stop for a moment, and re-read the quotation thus; I have italicized the words to make your task easier.

Some time ago I heard the Bishop of New York, Richard Grein, preaching in Washington Cathedral, tell the story of a friend of his who, when he is reading a mystery story, invariably turns first to the last chapter, "to read who done it". Asked why he did this, he replied: "If I know the end, I know all the clues. I don't have to look for them, they stand out. I see the whole. I like it better that way. Besides, that's the way they write these books. A good mystery writer always writes the end, and then writes the story to get to the end."

* (Quoted in John Henry Newman: *Prayers, Poems, Meditations*, by A. N. Wilson, S.P.C.K. 1989, p. 21).

Which is a parable of the way God deals with us in his Kingdom. As the Bishop said in his sermon: "God gives us the future in his plans. In the resurrection of Christ, the future is made present to us. . . ."

No one of us would dare to say "I know all the clues". The life of faith is not like that. As Newman said: "We are in a world of mystery." But in some measure to be able to "see the whole", to glimpse "the end" to which history is moving, to which *we* are moving, is a treasure of infinite worth. It is given to the man of faith, the person of hope, who refuses to believe with Macbeth that history is "a tale told by an idiot, full of sound and fury, signifying nothing". To be without that clue, without that Light, without that hope, is to be on the road to despair.

The alternative to the outlook of hope is a bleak one. Literature, and biography especially, provide us with ample material to see its dark outlines.

> 'Tis all a chequer-board of nights and days
> Where destiny with men for pieces plays;
> Hither and thither moves, and mates, and slays,
> And one by one back in the closet lays.

Poor Omar Khayyam! But he speaks for many at the close of the twentieth century as he spoke for many at the end of the eleventh. A modern musical, *Lost in the Stars*, puts that viewpoint with a moving pathos:

> A bird of passage out of night
>   Flies in at a lighted door,
> Flies through and on in its darkened flight
>   And then is seen no more.

This is the life of men on earth;
  Out of darkness we come at birth
Into a lamplit room, and then –
  Go forward into dark again,
Go forward into dark again.

There is nothing here of the violence of Dylan Thomas in the face of death:

  Do not go gentle into that good night,
  Old age should burn and rave at close of day;
  Rage, rage against the dying of the light.

Rather, the musical faces, bravely but bleakly, the reality of man's mortality, unilluminated by resurrection. Alan Paton, commenting on the author of these lines in *Lost in the Stars*, described him as "an unbeliever . . . not an atheist, and certainly not a militant one . . ." who "believed that there had been a Creator, and that he had gone away, leaving us lost out here in the stars". The author speaks for many.

"Out of darkness . . . forward into dark again." The concept haunts us, daunts us – I had almost said "taunts us". The immensity of the universe; the absurdity of our littleness; the sheer transitoriness of it all. . . .

It is significant that on the title page of J. B. Priestley's autobiography he quotes the lines from Shakespeare's *King Lear*:

                              men must endure
  Their going hence, even as their coming hither;
  Ripeness is all.

Priestley was a man tantalized by the problem of the "hereafter". Behind the "Jolly Jack Priestley" whom his friends enjoyed knowing, the Bradford lad made good, the much-read author and wartime broadcaster, was another Priestley who, despite his "theoretical belief in the libertarian values . . . could not entirely escape the penalties of his infidelities" (Vincent Brome: *J. B. Priestley*, Hamish Hamilton, 1988, p.161); a man who, in the long dark hours of sleepless nights, found himself "alone, completely alone, really feeling for once that you are imprisoned in your consciousness . . . a truly horrible glimpse of hell . . ." (p.387). At best, for Priestley "our going hence" must be "endured". Meanwhile, take what life offers. Here he is in New York: "Restless, uneasy, the impossibility of sitting still drove him out to see a show, eat and drink, mix with the crowds . . . take a river trip, go to the theatre, see the Rockefeller Center, find yourself a woman . . . and never face the horror of an unfulfilled empty space unpressurized by people or appointments. 'Time must not merely be killed but savagely murdered in public'." It could not last. Another phase broke in. " 'I could not sleep properly, began to feel tired, empty, desolated' " (p.159). A troubled sea; frenetic activity; no light; no clue; no peace at the centre; "forward into dark again".

A far greater writer than Priestley, Leo Tolstoy, found himself tortured by what he called "the hideous and inescapable fact of death" and the terrible pointlessness of existence. His latest biographer, A. N. Wilson, has told us how Tolstoy, during the closing stages of writing *Anna Karenina* "had to hide ropes and guns from himself for fear of yielding to temptation" (A. N.

Wilson: *Tolstoy*, Hamish Hamilton, 1988, p.272). "He was now unable to think of anything in life without realizing that all action, all feeling, all achievement, all desire would one day be swallowed up and rendered pointless by death. . . . We know that we have nothing to look forward to but death" (p.251). To watch such a man, who had given to the world literature that has about it the mark of immortality, at the end excommunicated by his church, his wife suspicious of his every move and herself mentally sick, facing a future which had no light in it – that is to see a spectacle of enormous tragedy. With insight, A. N. Wilson writes: "Tolstoy, who had been so awe-struck by the strange phenomenon of life ever since he had become conscious of his own existence, so sure of the fact that life was full of significance, had never been able to grasp what that significance was. Now, as it hastened to its close, few lives seemed more fuller than his own of sound and fury, signifying nothing" (p.511).

> At death, you break up; the bits that were you
> Start speeding away from each other for ever
> With no one to see –
>
> *(The Old Fools)*

Was Philip Larkin right? Tolstoy, had he been able to read the lines which Larkin was to write, might well have wondered, and said "Yes".

Macbeth, Omar Khayyam, Dylan Thomas, Priestley, Tolstoy, Larkin. In an article in the *Church Times* (26 January, 1990) the Archbishop of York, John Habgood, tells us of a recent event in his life when he rediscovered Browning. Near the end of his article he wrote: "I wish we had a Browning among us today. Most of our poets and playwrights seem to have a bleaker, sadder vision. And there is a distressingly one-dimensional feel about much public discussion of religious matters."

The words "bleak" and "sad" summarize what we have been saying in this chapter, and underline it. Of the "one-dimensional" element we shall have something to say later in this chapter. Meanwhile we need only ask: Can "bleakness" and "sadness" be far away if there is but one dimension to life, if the element of eternity be missing?

We readily admit that many lives have been lived nobly under the banner of that bleak creed. Many men and women, in spite of its cold cynicism, have made their contribution to the world they lived in and to the society of which they were a part. Perhaps, in some strange way, the very shortness of the life they lived and the finality of death as they saw it, added a certain urgency to the work they had to do: "Only one life, and that a brief one. Do what you can do, and do it well. Leave the world a better place than it was when you entered it. Then – out into the dark. Chins up!" We have all met such people, and our feeble Christian character has been rebuked by their kindness and their contribution to the lives of their contemporaries.

Nevertheless, it must be said that the person who puts a full-stop to life when the heart stops beating lays himself open to one or more enemy invaders. He will not necessarily succumb to them all, or totally to any one of them, but he is in danger.

If, to use the language of an earlier part of this chapter, we have no light, no clue, no vision of the "whole", no glimpse of the End towards which life here moves, we can easily become victims of that frenetic *activism* of which, so his biographer suggests, Priestley was an example. "Life is short – then every hour must be filled; every flavour sampled; every excitement seized upon. Silence should be avoided – keep the radio on; don't turn off the television." Frenetic activism is the opposite of the peace which comes to those who believe in a God whose plan is not thwarted by the incident of physical dissolution.

Giant *despair*, too, stands at the ready to invade the person with no hope of a life to come. Its cousin cynicism is not far off. (Tolstoy provides us with an illustration). Very often this invasion is accompanied by an acquisitiveness which says: "Make what you can while you can; you can't take it with you." The hollowness of such a philosophy is patent for all to see – if we were not blind. But in individual lives, and in the political economy of nations, the falseness of this philosophy dies hard; it rears its ugly head with surprising vitality. Japan can make a good claim to be the most "prosperous" nation on earth; yet its suicide rate is said to be the highest in the world. Hedonism, the pursuit of pleasure as being the highest good, is attractive, but follow its ways and the taste in your mouth is bitter. Isaiah accused his nation of self-indulgence at a time when repentance was their greatest need. No, said his compatriots: "Let us eat and drink, for tomorrow we die!" (22:13). Paul quotes the saying in the context of those who hold the view that "the dead are never raised to life" and who relapse into a life of hedonism (1 Corinthians 15:32).

"The opposite of the virtue of hope is the vice of despair" (John Macquarrie, *Christian Hope*, p.10). Apathy, indifference, inaction follow in its wake. Whereas hope stimulates action, despair saps it, leaving a vacuum, an emptiness, a sense of futility. The victim of despair is drained of his vitality.

The problems which we have been considering are pin-pointed for us in an excruciating form by the sufferings of the Jewish people in the holocaust. So appalling was Hitler's attempt at the destruction of a race, genocide at its worst, that we may speak of *"the* holocaust" without further definition and be understood. There have been many holocausts in the long saga of man's inhumanity to man. But the murder of six million Jews at the behest of one man during the Second World War makes this terrible act unique.

The Jewish people have been, *par excellence*, the people of hope. Chapter 1 of this book is a study of *Jewish* writings. It was their prophets and poets who taught us how to hope and began to point us to the God in whom to put our hope. Jesus, the Man of hope, sprang from that race (chapter 2). And the messages of hope in the writings of the New Testament flowed, almost all of them, from Jewish pens (chapter 3). Ever since the holocaust, some half-century ago, theologians, Jewish and Christian, have wrestled with the problems presented by it. Indeed it has given rise to a considerable body of "holocaust theology". Where was God at Auschwitz? That is to put the problem in a nutshell and at its starkest. *There* is the challenge of theodicy in its sternest colours – how can one defend the attributes of a God of love and mercy against the obscenities of the gas chambers?

This is no place to argue the case for the presence of God in the prison camps – or his absence from them. But something must be said particularly about the *Jewish* response to the problem – rather, we should say "responses", for they have been, and continue to be, many and various.

At the heart of a devout Jew's faith is his belief in a God of loving mercy who enters into a covenant-relationship with his people; a God, moreover, who is a God of justice and of judgement, who holds nations and individuals, made in his image, responsible for their actions towards him and towards their fellow-men. His relationship to the Jewish people was one of special intimacy, for to them he had given a revelation of unique quality. Moreover, he had given them a *land* – "the earth is the Lord's", and they are trustees responsible to him for their use or misuse of it.

This lofty and at the same time down-to-earth theology itself sharpens the problem presented by Auschwitz and Belsen. Millions of Jews, tortured (some more, some less), despaired of a solution to the problem and abandoned their faith and relapsed into various forms of atheism, nihilism, hedonism. (Christians can in no way condemn them for that, for millions of Gentiles, faced with this kind of problem, have reacted in a similar way. The problem is no less for the Christian than it is for the Jew; indeed, some would say it is even sharper for the Christian who believes that in the Messiah Jesus the heart and mind of God have been disclosed to mankind in a unique way.)

Other Jews have not been content to leave it at that – they have continued to wrestle. In a book more valuable than its size might suggest, Rabbi Dan Cohn-Sherbok has outlined the attempts which some of his most thoughtful fellow-Jews have made to shed some light on the darkness (*Holocaust Theology*, Lamp Press, Marshall Morgan & Scott, 1989). One sees God, not indeed as being absent from the camps, but present and acting in wrath directed at a people who had neglected his Torah and forgotten their faith. Only when they have been thus purified will they return to their land and the spark of Judaism will be re-kindled. Another sees light on the problem by concentrating on the Suffering Servant concept. Destruction left a saving remnant and that remnant must speak "with the Hallelujah of the redeemed at the Red Sea". So the attempts go on – part cries of agony, all attempts at justifying the mysterious ways of God with his creation. We Gentiles can only seek with reverence to share in the agony of the search.

For many Jews – perhaps we should say for most Jews – their hope has been centred in the Land. I spell it with a capital, for the concept of a Land, given in days long gone to a people of God's choice, a Land every foot of which is peculiarly their own, to be treasured, to be occupied and used with reverence, this is something tangible, visual, actual in everyday living. "*Here* is our hope," cry Jews of widely different backgrounds and widely differing beliefs and of no "belief" at all. "To this Land we can now return. In it we can live in peace, and raise our children and renew our life.

We may not be able to put much faith in the God of our fathers; but we believe in the Land. *This* is our hope."

Again we Gentiles have no right to assume an attitude of superiority, for millions of our people are just as "materialistic" in their approach to life. The acquisitive society, with its emphasis on money and on things rather than on mercy and on people, can ill sit in judgement on others who put their trust in the *Land*. Great numbers who would be insulted if the title "Christian" was not allowed them, do little about reaching a lively faith of their own. And if they were asked what they mean when they recite that article of the Creed which declares "I believe . . . in the life of the world to come", they would be able to do little more than stutter and relapse into silence.

For such, Jews and Gentiles alike, "hope" is entirely – or almost entirely – mundane in the literal sense of the word, this-earth centred. The concept of another world, of a hope centred in the beyond, of a life to come when this material existence is no more, of a future judgement and the possibility of a great Assize – this is entirely beyond them. It is a territory so far divorced from all that they conceive of as reality, that it is not worth entering, still less exploring. "Our hope is in the here and now" – full stop.

But for many others, Jews and Gentiles alike, this just will not do. This is true of Jews as well as of Gentiles. Rabbi Cohn-Sherbok is one of the most thoughtful of those Jews who are not satisfied with any attempt to find light on the problem purely on a this-worldly plane. Having examined the attempts of six Jewish theologians and found them wanting, he concludes his book with a final chapter entitled "The Holocaust and the Afterlife". "One element is missing from all these justifications of Jewish suffering: there is no appeal to the Hereafter." That is the nub of his complaint. He points out that "Life after Death came into prominence during the Maccabaean period when righteous individuals were dying for their faith." We have already noted this (see pp.34–36). He maintains that such a faith has been a tenet of the Jewish belief from that period onwards. "The World to Come in which justice would be done and be seen to be done was a necessary part of the Jewish scheme of things." (We might add that precisely the same may and must be said of the Christian faith.) In the Middle Ages thousands of Jews lost their lives in battle or by suicide for their faith, and they did so "fortified by the belief that God would redeem them in a future life". A similar belief nourished the courage of many Jews when the Nazis were oppressing them – "What can they do to me?" asked an old Jew. "They can take my body but not my soul. Over the soul they have no authority. Here they are powerful. But in the Other World they are powerless." Another Jew, Yossell Rakover from the Warsaw ghetto, left a letter before he died: "In an hour at most I will be with my wife and children and with millions of people who died, in that better world, where God rules alone. . . . May he be praised for ever, the God of the dead, the God of vengeance, the God of truth and justice, who will again light his Countenance on the world. Hear O Israel, the Lord our God, the Lord is One. In your hand I place my soul."

Dan Cohn-Sherbok would argue that to abandon, or

to lose hold on, that great concept of a world to come and a judgement to come is to share in a major shift of orientation. Devotion to the Land, however intense that devotion may be, is not the same thing as, nor can it take the place of a forward look, a forward faith, a future hope. The State of Israel can never be a substitute for the Messiah himself, nor can secular Zionism, nor can belief in the continuity of Jewish peoplehood; nor for that matter can a belief in the immortality of the soul take the place of the doctrine of the resurrection of the dead. "Without this belief, it is simply impossible to make sense of the world as the creation of an all-good and all-powerful God." His view is corroborated by another Jew, Professor Irving Greenberg: "The moral necessity of a world to come, and even of resurrection, arises powerfully out of encounter with the Holocaust" (quoted by Marcus Braybrooke: *Time to Meet*, S.C.M., 1990, p.117).

Among Christian writers who have sought to grapple with the possibility of hope when so much around us points in the direction of despair is J. Christiaan Beker. In his book *Suffering and Hope* (Fortress Press, Philadelphia, 1987), he writes against the background of his imprisonment in a German forced labour camp. He confesses that his experience of struggling with the issue of suffering has led him to the conviction "that the only realistic hope a Christian can cherish, if he or she is not to succumb to despair, is the apocalyptic hope in God's eventual triumph over the power of death" (p.10). In this, Christian thinker and Jewish Rabbi are at one.

But Beker goes on, as must any Christian who looks back at the cross and resurrection of Jesus, to point us to the fact "that God has intervened in his perverted world and has created a new world where the power of idolatry with its attendant suffering has been overcome." And he sees the Church as representing this new world, itself "the beachhead and vanguard of God's saving design for his creation", inserted into the old creation "by God's grace in order to exhibit a new form of life and to found a new basis for human hope and fulfilment" (pp.62, 63). Karl Barth had made much the same point about the Church when he spoke of it as "God's provisional demonstration of his intention for all humanity", and Lesslie Newbigin when he spoke of it as "the sign, instrument, and foretaste of God's Kingdom". But for our purpose Beker's description will serve – "the beachhead and vanguard of God's saving design for his creation".

Who would dare to say that the love and imagination of God were exhausted?

To hope is a duty, not a luxury. To hope is not to dream, but to turn dreams into reality.

Happy are those who dream dreams and are ready to pay the price to make them come true.

Cardinal Suenens

5

Messengers of Hope

"The Church as the beachhead and vanguard of God's saving design for his creation" – this is a magnificent concept. The Church as a body of men and women who look back to God's saving intervention in what we have called the Christ-event, and who look forward in faith and hope to the consummation, the End towards which history moves at the beckoning of God – this is an enlivening concept. And it is one which is renewed at every Eucharist – "till he come".

We are the *interim*-people, implicated in the griefs of this present world, as was our incarnate Lord, never pulling out from them but always sharing in the groanings and yearnings of creation, and, at the same time, on the tiptoe of expectancy for the day when "he shall reign". And if, between the backward look and the forward look we are stretched to the limit (racked?), what matter? In the very stretching is the power.

There is much that puzzles and perplexes us in a world beset by suffering. No thoughtful Christian can go to the world with a trite and easy word, "all buttoned-up". The quotation of odd Bible texts, after the pattern of American tele-evangelists, will not do. But if, in the midst of our doubtings and our tremblings, we look to the crucified and risen Christ as the ground of our hope, and to the Kingdom of God as its horizon, we may – indeed we must – go to a despairing world as *messengers of hope*.

We must expect to be misunderstood. The world as we know it puts what hope it has in *power* and its tactics, the power of arms, the power of money, the power of sex, the power of arm-twisting. Jesus knows no such power – only the power of self-giving love. "Force is no attribute of God," says the Epistle to Diognetus. "God exercises his power in relation to men through self-giving and service"*, and his servants can know no other way. That to the world will seem folly, but the supreme self-giving on Calvary met the same estimate from the powers that were. We follow in Christ's steps.

Nevertheless, there are signs abroad that, in some areas at least, the world is looking to the Church – is it in desperation? – for some evidence that it, too, is grappling with the "nonsense" of a society which is largely post-Christian, and that the Church has a contribution to make.

The brilliant Jewish novelist, Chaim Potok, believes because "God is no longer accepted as the one central, dominant, overarching Being in our society", we must look to the artist to give shape to the world. "The artist is . . . an icon in his own right, a god without a capital G. . . ." "For now", he says, "there is no clear line

---

* *Suffering: A test of theological method*. By Arthur C. McGill, (Westminster Press, Philadelphia, 1982, p.79) – a stimulating study, in which redemption is defined as liberation from satanic power and possession by the power of God.

of vertical authority to give shape to the world. . . . Everything is horizontal, on a par. . . ." (*Jewish Chronicle Literary Supplement*, 10th August 1990). There he has pin-pointed modern man's dilemma.

In similar vein, Charles Pickstone, in an article on the visual theology of Vincent Van Gogh (in *Theology*, July/August 1990), writes of the artist's "secular spirituality. There are no religious symbols and there is no transcendent deity in [the paintings] to create order out of strife. . . ." He goes on: "One of Vincent's last pictures, 'Wheatfield with Crows', shows the complete disintegration into which he was falling. There is no centre. Three paths lead out of the picture in different directions, the flight of the crows (harbingers of death) towards the viewer provides yet another axis. *There are no vertical lines*, only infinite horizontals stretching out to engulf the viewer. *Without the vertical of transcendence, the world falls in on itself*" (italics mine).

Writer (Potok) and painter (Van Gogh) both lament the absence of the dimension of the vertical.

Benedict Nightingale, in a recent article in *The Times* (8 August 1990), asks "whether our playwrights have been shirking their spiritual responsibilities". Samuel Beckett, "an agnostic going on atheist . . . yet dedicated his career to considering what it means to be a human maybug in a vast and seemingly uncaring universe". He at least had "a metaphysical mindset". But "Harold Pinter's most powerful works leave the impression that, behind the social pretence, we human animals are doomed to spend our lives battling for territory, sex, dominance and power. He is the Charles Darwin of our theatre, a philosopher-dramatist for whom the world is a godless jungle in which only the fittest survive." Nightingale sees (and protests against) "an unwritten agreement among our most serious dramatists to forget philosophical issues and concentrate on political or private ones; to take the cosmos for granted, and concern themselves with social justice, personal relationships, and other matters obviously close to home. All else seems to them irrelevant and vaguely embarrassing." Nightingale cannot rest there: "The mind longs for larger perspectives." He suggests that the present revival on the stage of *King Lear* is because "of all plays, it asks the hardest, deepest questions about what its characters call 'the gods'. Could it be that it answers a craving unsatisfied elsewhere?"

Nightingale's questions should give the messengers of hope furiously to think. Out of the corner of his eye, in this thoughtful article the author is looking at "the Church of England, or any other religious institution. . . . Spiritual food is what it is fundamentally in business to serve." By implication, I believe he would ask whether, in fact, the Church itself is seeking to deal with the deepest issues ("the gods"), to meet that "craving unsatisfied elsewhere", or is it content to deal with lesser issues, the more immediate matters which clamour for attention? The question is a deeply serious one. Are the messengers of hope consistently pointing to the God of hope, the fountain of living water, or are they content to seek to quench their people's thirst at "cisterns, cracked cisterns, which hold no water" (Jeremiah 2:13)? Are our teaching, preaching, living,

God-centred? What did Van Gogh's picture tell us? "Without the vertical of transcendence, the world falls in on itself."

Run the eye of your memory over the last few sermons which you heard in your local church (or, which you preached in your local church). Were those sermons mostly concerned with the vertical or with the horizontal? A recent writer notes "a tendency in the Church to replace theology by ecclesiology – God has become low on the agenda while the Church itself has become the focus of attention" That is bad enough, for such a tendency, if maintained, will lead to an inward-looking Church, and that in turn leads to death.

But there is another "tendency in the Church" which is, perhaps, fraught with even greater peril, not least because of its subtlety. It is the tendency to concentrate on the social implications of the Gospel as if they were the Gospel itself. This, again, is to concentrate on the horizontal rather than the vertical. *Of course*, the horizontal matters; the messengers of hope are the sons and daughters of the *incarnate* Lord, and they must never let up on the down-to-earth social issues on which, as the successors of the prophets, they have a word of the Lord to declare.

I repeat, the horizontal matters. But I ask: Are we concentrating on it to the detriment of the vertical? To put it more pointedly and to pin it more locally: Do the worshippers in our churches go away from them, at the end of a service, with an overwhelming sense that they have met with *God* in the worship, meditated on *God* in the sermon and the silences; encountered *God* in his holiness and his grace? In what direction have their eyes mostly turned – upwards? or outwards and inwards?

We can be easily misunderstood on this matter. A few decades ago it used to be said of Christians in this country that they were so heavenly-minded that they were of no earthly use. There was much to justify that accusation. The social conscience of the Church was slovenly, slothful. The iniquities and the inequities of society did not seem to register on the so-called Christian conscience of many churchgoers. The result was that people voted with their feet and absented themselves from what seemed to them to be an un-caring, even hypocritical, body of believers.

In some areas, that attitude – be it said to our shame – still persists. But by and large the picure has altered. Social issues are high on the Church's agenda. And rightly so – the horizontal matters. But the pendulum has a way of swinging – and it has swung. In many areas, as we may judge from much preaching and writing, the emphasis has moved so greatly to the horizontal that the vertical is well-nigh eliminated. The charge now might be made – and with too much justification for our comfort – that the Church is so earthly-minded that it is of no heavenly use. And that, if true, could lead to the removal of its candle from its place.

Prebendary D. W. Cleverley Ford has sounded a warning note: "Of course we have little time for those men and women so preoccupied with their piety, that they have no place in their hearts for the unfortunate, the broken, and certainly none for the weak-willed of the world of whom there are plenty. If, however, the modern Church has nothing else for which to call than better housing, better medical facilities, better pensions and jobs for all, it has no claim to be heard above the other charitable organizations which cover this ground." He goes on to ask: If the Church has nothing much to *say* when faced with such tragedies as the Channel ferry disaster, the Armenian earthquake, the Pan-Am Lockerbie devastation, "what is the special ground of its existence?" (*Preaching on the Holy Spirit*, Mowbray, 1990, pp.62–3). The world has a right to look to the Church for guidance, when its own gods are only leading them to cynicism and even despair. The horizontal and the temporal never satisfy men and women made for the vertical and the eternal.

Recently, Dr Maurice M. Benitez, Bishop of Texas, addressed the Church Club of New York. He tried to get his hearers to face the condition of the Episcopal Church in the United States: "Why are people going out the back door faster than they are coming in the front door? What have we been doing wrong?" He put his first answer to the problem very forcefully: "We . . . have been excessively focused on social and political concerns. Food pantries, ministry to the homeless, outreach projects, protesting apartheid in South Africa, fighting racism, sexism and all forms of injustice. These are all good things, they are important Christian concerns, they are vital ministries, but they are not the Gospel. They are a by-product of people hearing the Gospel, becoming disciples of Jesus Christ and trying to live Christ-centred lives. They are not a substitute for the Gospel." The Bishop went on to ask: "Why are we so embarrassed to witness to our faith in Jesus

Christ, to offer them also our most precious possession, the gift of eternal life?"

Again, run the eye of your memory over recent sermons you have heard in your church (or which you preached in your church). Most of them were concerned – and rightly so – with issues of everyday life (seen, we may hope, under the searchlight of the Gospel). But did any of those sermons deal with *death* and what comes after it? I have to die – and so have you. Will someone tell me about death and how to face it? If I can find no one within the Church to do this, where else am I to go?

I notice that at funeral and memorial services, it has become popular to read some words of Henry Scott Holland (Canon of St Paul's Cathedral, London, from 1884 till 1910 when he became Regius Professor of Divinity at Oxford):

> Death is nothing at all; I have only slipped away into the next room. I am I and you are you; whatever we were to each other we are still. Call me by my old familiar name; speak to me in the easy way which we always used. Put no difference into your tone; wear no forced air of solemnity or sorrow. Laugh, as we always laughed at the little jokes together. Pray, smile, think of me, pray for me. . . . Life means all that it ever meant; it is the same as it ever was; there is absolute unbroken continuity. What is this death but a negligible accident? Why should I be out of mind because I am out of sight? I am but waiting for you, for an interval, somewhere very near, just around the corner. All is well.

There is much of comfort here, and it must be remembered that the words were written against the background of the First World War, when the writer was seeking to console the hearts of those bereaved people who came to hear him. But will it do? Is this all that we have to say in the face of man's last enemy? As we read the pages of the New Testament, we shall not find death dealt with in so trivial a fashion. There is evidence to show that Jesus spoke of it with far greater seriousness. Is not death, in the great Christian tradition, rather to be regarded as an enemy, but one whose sting has been drawn by the death and resurrection of the Son of God? "Just as it is our human lot to die once, with judgement to follow, so Christ was offered once to bear the sins of mankind . . ." (Hebrews 9:27). The language may be difficult for a modern reader to understand, but at least he is faced with realities which call for his serious attention. The Pauline writings focus on "the appearance on earth of our Saviour Jesus Christ" who "has broken the power of death and brought life and immortality to light through the Gospel" (2 Timothy 1:10). The collect of Easter day is close to the biblical writings when it speaks of the "Lord of all life and power who through the mighty resurrection of your Son overcame the old order of sin and death to make all things new in him".

Is not the fact of death in itself a call to the Church to be faithful to these realities – to face death, but always in the light of Christ's death and resurrection and of the possibility of incorporation into the new order of life and light? To what other place of hope can the Church point the people than to the love of God in Christ Jesus our Lord, a love stronger than death itself?

The messengers of hope, if they are to be true to their title, must go back, again and again, to that which others cannot give – the God of hope, the Man of hope, the message of hope (at once this-worldly and other-worldly), the expectancy of hope. Only so will their message be like that of the prophets, "shining like a lamp in a murky place, until day breaks . . ." (2 Peter 1:19).

What should be the stance of the messengers of hope as they come into contact with those who have no such specific hope or who, perhaps very regretfully, feel that they cannot themselves lay hold of it? Needless to say, the Christian man or woman of hope must take care never to evidence – no, never to *feel* – any sense of superiority. If he has, however feebly, begun to lay hold of that hope which is like an anchor of the soul, that is only by God's gracious mercy. Nor can he be dismissive of the other man's hopes, however frail he (the Christian) may think them to be. Let us illustrate this from the standpoint of recent events:

All who read this book will remember to the end of their days the surge of hope which flowed over Europe with the end of the cold war, the advent of *glasnost* and *perestroika*, the removal of the Berlin wall, the human touch of Gorbachev. The log-jam in international relations was breaking up. The prospect of a united Europe was bright. In all this, the messengers of hope were, we trust, the first to rejoice. Wherever truth prevails over error, wherever compassion wins over hate, wherever beauty ousts ugliness, *there*, they argue, is the work of the Holy Spirit, even though some of the agents of this liberation may be unconscious of his presence and activity in them. The messengers of hope would go further. They would argue that such good things as we have just mentioned are themselves signs of God's Kingdom at work in our midst: the light is chasing the darkness, the yeast is doing its work in society. The reign of God which came in unique power in the person of Jesus Christ has been at work from that day until now – its effervescent presence and its powerful action are in evidence throughout the world, constituting as they do the basis of the hope that the Day will come when all opposition to God's reign will cease and with its cessation there will be an end to our crying and our tears.

So the messengers of hope welcome these miracles of which we would not have dreamed even a few years ago. God is at work! Where next will he move? What further surprises has he in store for us? At the same time, the Christian is a realist. He knows something of "the mystery of iniquity" which is always at work, and of the havoc which sin is wreaking in the hearts and minds of men. He shares in the agony of Bernard Levin who, in a leading article in *The Times* (2 January 1989) which was something of a *cri de coeur*, asked: "Is there some kind of entropy in societies, so that the more they advance in technology, wealth, confidence, even *civilitas*, the more rapidly the degeneration of humanity's essence goes on?" And Levin asks: "*Must* I join the pessimists?" The messengers of hope appreciate the questions. But they know the folly of putting one's trust in anyone or anything other than God. Almost wistfully Levin writes: "I know what Solzhenitsyn would say, because he says it: 'Man has forgotten God.' Perhaps: anyway, man has forgotten *something*. . . ." The Christian is not a cynic, but he is aware that all history tells him that to put your trust in "Egypt" – that Old Testament name for Godless power – is like leaning your weight on a splintered cane: you will only find that it leaves you with a bloody hand (Isaiah 36:6).

The Christian is not a cynic; nor is he a pessimist. His vision of the power of the risen Christ and of the ultimate triumph of the Kingdom wherein dwells righteousness prevents him from ever becoming *that*, however dark the clouds may be. No: he is a proximate realist and an ultimate optimist (see p.55). All his hope on *God* is founded. His feet are firmly on the ground, while his eyes look forward to the Day. The fight is still on and he is in the thick of it. The enemy is powerful and subtle, but in the Christian's heart is a song. He remembers the word of Paul: "Let hope keep you joyful; in trouble stand firm" (Romans 12:12).

Realist that he is, he has no faith in the doctrine of human progress. That philosophy, if such it may be called, so popular at the beginning of the twentieth century, received its death-blow with the two World Wars, though the idea re-emerges from time to time with an uncanny vigour. Based in America, that land of wealth and plenty, J. Christiaan Beker recently referred to "our deeply routinized assumption of technological, educational, and social progress". He went on: "In fact, the concept of the world as a steady evolution to better conditions of life has formed and still forms the natural house of meaning for many of us. Is not this the reason behind our celebration of American culture as unique on earth? Isn't this what makes us vote for politicians who promise us unending hopes of prosperity and growth? But now, underneath the surface, we are slowly forced to surrender this doctrine of progress, prosperity, and increasing abundance" (*Suffering and Hope*, p.19). That is a surrender much to be welcomed. Jeremiah had made the point centuries before Christ in a pungent warning: "Let not the wise boast of their wisdom, nor the valiant of their valour; let not the wealthy boast of their wealth; but if anyone must boast, let him boast of this: that he understands and acknowledges me. For I am the Lord . . ." (9:23,24).

A danger which constantly assails the Church is to "think small", when the Christian revelation bids us "think big". We narrow the horizons of the Christian hope – it is easier that way. But so to narrow them is to miss the splendour of the Christian hope. When, in the General Thanksgiving, we bless God for "the hope of glory", is that an individualistic hope? Yes: but *so much more*. The bishops who attended the Lambeth Conference in 1988 were not content with such a limitation. When they spoke of "the ultimate goal" – they were dealing specifically with the matter of *unity* – they said these wise words: "The ultimate goal" (we might say "the Christian hope") "is not simply the unity of the Church. It is a gift which comes into the world from God and which will be completely revealed only at the end of time. It is the perfect reign of God over a reconciled, restored and transformed creation. It will be a Kingdom in which what has been broken, distorted or disordered by the sin of men and women will be mended and put right through the life, death and resurrection of Jesus Christ. What is to be put right is not only a shattered humanity . . . but also the whole universe . . . It is to be a consummation of the work of Jesus Christ. In his earthly ministry Jesus released people from slavery, healed the sick, forgave sins, fed the hungry, cast out devils, and pointed to those actions as signs that the final victory over the powers of evil was assured and that the Kingdom or rule of God had already begun. The Kingdom which he inaugurated in his earthly ministry will be completed at the end of time . . ." (*The Lambeth Conference, 1988: The Reports, Resolutions and Pastoral Letters from the Bishops*, p.131).

In sending this message to the world, the Lambeth Fathers were clearly indebted to the thinking of Paul. The classic passage in which he wrestles with the subject of cosmic hope is in Romans 8:18ff. As I have written elsewhere: "Though he did not put it in these terms, [Paul] believed that God, having set his hand to the creation of his universe, would not look back till his purpose in and for that creation was realized. 'The creation waits . . .' 'We to whom the Spirit has been given . . . wait.' We live in the era of 'not yet', of hope so far only partially fulfilled; but we live in the knowledge that God is co-operating for good with those who love him, who cannot be separated from his love by any power in the universe. On the grand scale, Paul saw the *universe*, created through Christ and for Christ, reconciled through Christ to the Father . . ." (*Paul: Portrait of a Revolutionary*, pp. 186–7). "It was with this hope that we were saved . . . We look forward to it eagerly and with patience," says Paul (Romans 8:24–5).

Christ is not only "head of the body, the Church" (Colossians 1:18); "his is the primacy over all creation" (v.15). "The universe, everything in heaven and on earth" is to "be brought into a unity in Christ" (Ephesians 1:10).

Christ is himself at once the foretaste and the pledge of the great consummation, the End to which all creation moves. In him "God has, as it were, unmistakably shown his hand, has unveiled further his purposes in the cosmos and the meaning he has written in man" (A. R. Peacocke: *Creation and the World of Science*, pp. 244–5). We may heed the testimony of J. C. Beker: "The Christian hope in the ultimate triumph of God over the poisonous reality of death and its attendant suffering is compelling to me because of its cosmic – all embracing – dimension" (op. cit., p.11). In that light, "preoccupation with the *human* is beginning to sound distressingly parochial".

Perhaps that is about as far as we can go. We are finite beings, limited by the concepts of time and space, dealing with matters which defy precise definition. But to seek to climb the heights with a thinker such as Paul and so to attain a greater sense of the hope set before us is to gain a sense of proportion which can steady nerve and strengthen resolve.

Julien Green, the latest biographer of Francis of Assisi, tells us how, looking back over the period of his research, he noted that Francis' life had taken place "almost at the midpoint between the first Christmas and the hell humanity was writhing in" (the Second World War). "But he too had failed." Then he went on: "Failed? Apparently . . . He was convinced that salvation would come through the Gospel. The Gospel was eternity, the Gospel had only just begun. What were twenty centuries in the eyes of God?" (*God's Fool: The Life and Times of Francis of Assisi*. Harper and Row, English Translation, 1985). I combine these words of Julien Green's with a sentence recently spoken to me with great conviction by a wise messenger of hope. Lunch was over; we had been putting the world to rights, not without striking some minor notes. As we rose to go on our ways he said: "I never lose heart while there is the Gospel." I would want to add, as no doubt would he: "While there is the Holy Spirit," for he is the great *Animateur*, the Enlivener. The Gospel has only just begun!

If we need not despair of God's purpose for his *universe* – he is able to do a new thing, even to create "new heavens and a new earth, in which justice will be established" (2 Peter 3:13) – what are we to say about the *Church*? Here is the point of despair for many serious people. I am not thinking of those – and they are many – who make the Church's failures a facile *excuse* for their taking no part in its worship and work. I am thinking of people who have not abandoned the Church though they have been sore tempted to do so, and of others who have left it but with very sore hearts. And sometimes most of us who love the Church and realize something of the debt which we owe to the "mother" who has borne us and nourished us – sometimes we have blurted out, in a distress which springs from love: "Must not God sometimes despair of his Church?"

We see the Church's sinfulness and weakness – there

are evidences all around us. Disunity – pride – self-interest – competitiveness – lack of zeal; it would not take much intelligence to lengthen the list. How can this broken Body be "the beachhead and vanguard of God's saving design for his creation"? What do we hold on to, in moments when the cloud of the Church's sins threatens to blot out the radiance of its achievements and tempt us to despair? We lift our eyes from the horizontal to the vertical!

"Christ *loved* the Church and gave himself up for it," so Paul affirms (Ephesians 5:25). In as much as love knows no dying, we may change Paul's tense and say: "Christ *loves* the Church." Love loves the unlovable. Paul wrote to a group of churches which were no impeccable models of what the Church should be; on the contrary, they were marked by all kinds of nastiness. But "Christ loves the Church." That is of the nature of love – not to wait till the object of that love is perfect, but in the depths of unloveliness, to go on loving it. Paul does not leave it there. Christ might have been tempted to abandon the Church. On the contrary – he "gave himself up for it, to consecrate and cleanse it by water and word". Why? Because he had a vision for its future – a Day when that Church would be "all glorious, with no stain or wrinkle or anything of that sort, but holy and without blemish" (v.27).

That day is not yet. We, sinful members of a sinning Church, are *in the interim*. We may not run away from the fact that the Body of Christ is broken and bloody – indeed we ourselves are in part responsible for its brokenness and its bloodiness. We may not disassociate ourselves from that Church. Rather, we share in the consecrating and cleansing of it on which Christ is now engaged and will be till the end of time. And we share in the vision of the Day when it shall be "all glorious, with no stain or wrinkle . . .". Ours are the agony and the ecstasy, as they are his too.

Meanwhile we are encouraged by signs all around us of God's power in re-vivifying his Church. Just when it seems to be at its lowest, new shoots of life spring up. Old truths take on new life. New aspects of truth emerge – things which our fathers scarcely glimpsed become evident to their sons and daughters. The Church is growing up in its grasp of truth – East being taught by the insights of West, West by the insights of East, youth being taught by the wisdom of age, age being stimulated by the liveliness of youth – always advancing towards the plenitude of divine truth. "There is much more that I could say to you, but the burden would be too great for you now" – that was the situation before the cross, the resurrection and Pentecost. "However, when the Spirit of truth comes, he will guide you into all the truth . . ." (John 16:12–13). He has come: he is always coming; he will continue to come upon his Church, revealing, illuminating, enlivening. "Idolatry is essentially the worship of a static God," George Macleod used to tell his traditionalist friends. "Our God is a God that moves. The paradox of his changelessness is that he is in constant motion" (Ronald Ferguson: *George MacLeod: Founder of the Iona Community*, Collins, 1990, p.313). "God is on the side of that which is coming into being," George Cockin used to teach us. That is why his children should always be expectant of new truths, on the look-out for things hitherto unseen.

"We believe in the Lord, the Life-giver," the Lord who is wind and fire; and because we do so, we expect, we hope for (even if, because of our timidity, we sometimes fear) his inbreakings, his interruptions, his disturbance, his cauterizing, his revelation. We are the people of hope, *open to what may be*, open to what we may be drawn into, open for the next stage of our pilgrimage, living for the future which has begun in the here and now.

A perspective such as this provides us with an incentive in our worship, in our outreach, in our daily living, in our dying. It may seem a far cry from the immensities with which we have been wrestling in this chapter to the details of worship in St Agatha-in-the-Wallops or, for that matter, the worship in York Minster and Canterbury Cathedral. But that is not so. The quality of worship offered by a half-dozen men and women in a tiny church or by a great Cathedral congregation is related to Christ's "consecrating and cleansing" of the Church. It matters, therefore, whether that worship is full of awe and wonder or whether it is casual and sloppy; it matters whether there is time allowed for silence or whether there is an hour's bombardment of sound; it matters whether there is people-participation or a monologue on the part of the officiant; it matters whether the preaching is a declaration of God's grace or a few casual ideas thought up on Saturday night. Whether there be ten worshippers present or a thousand is irrelevant. That service is a participation by the worshippers in the ongoing worship of almighty God – we "chip in" with angels and archangels and all the company of heaven in the never-ending worship of God which is the primary function of his Church. That service, held in stately Cathedral or in village church or under a tree in Africa is pointing forward to the day when the Church, finally consecrated and cleansed, will need "no temple . . . the throne of God and of the Lamb will be there and his servants shall worship him; they shall see his face and bear his name on their foreheads" (Revelation 21:22; 22:3–4). *The perspective highlights the hope*.

What about the Church's *outreach*, the second main purpose of its existence? The perspectives of which we have been thinking prove to be an incentive here, too. The Church on earth is engaged in a battle against sin, ignorance and disease, against anything which mars the restoration of the image of God in which men and women are made. It is a desperate conflict to which the language of the "demonic", so familiar to the New Testament writers, seems to be assuming a horrible relevance in modern times. Against the in-coming tide of sin we raise the saving name of Jesus; against the tide of ignorance we do our teaching work; against the tide of sickness, we pit the forces of Christian "whole-ness". Often the tide bids fair to overwhelm us, but we go on. And then –

When the strife is fierce, the warfare long,
Steals on the ear the distant triumph-song,
And hearts are brave again and arms are strong.
                                                            Alleluia!

The perspective highlights the hope.
What about *daily living*? And what about *dying*?

Here again, intimately and personally, the perspective highlights the hope. In the General Thanksgiving, we bless God "for the means of grace, and *for the hope of glory*". According to the teaching of the New Testament, man's "glory", his creation in the image of God, has been marred and defaced by sin. When a human being finds himself put right with God, a process of "glorification" begins in him. This happens in the here and now. The re-creative life of God is operative within him. A process has begun whose fulfilment will only be reached when the confines of this little life are transcended. So "the hope of glory" is *this*-worldly as well as *that*-worldly.

To realize that God is now at work in a person, restoring his image, is to add a sense of dignity and significance to his daily living. The menial task takes on a splendour which, without such a hope, would be entirely lacking. George Herbert puts it well:

> All may of thee partake;
> Nothing can be so mean
> Which, with this tincture, *for thy sake*,
> Will not grow bright and clean.

> A servant with this clause
> Makes drudgery divine;
> Who sweeps a room, as for thy laws,
> Makes that and the action fine.

There can, however, be little doubt that when Bishop E. Reynolds composed the General Thanksgiving in 1661, he had in mind the future aspect of this "hope of glory". In "the means of grace" we are thanking God for pilgrim-provision. In "the hope of glory" we are looking to the time when such means of grace will be needed no more and sacraments will cease. We are thinking of the other side of dying, of life after death.

It is strange how reticent, even nervous or fearful, people are of speaking about death. If the Victorians were shy of speaking of sex, their late twentieth-century successors are equally shy of speaking of death. It is a bogey in the cupboard, of which less said, or even thought, the better. So, instead of saying "when I die", we say "if anything should happen to me". What folly! Of course it will happen. The one certainty is that death comes to us all. Perhaps the silence is understandable when it comes from those who have no hope, who look on death as an exit into the unknown and the end of everything.

A recent issue of *The Times* (January 19, 1991) had a *Profile* of an eminent businessman aged fifty-two. He spoke very frankly to his interviewer not only about his business successes and losses but also about his future. The recent death of his mother had touched him deeply. Generally he refuses to talk about it – and about his retirement. "I don't know what I'm going to do when I retire. I hate the idea of getting old. Death and getting old are big events in my life. I don't like to think about them. I'm scared of dying ... I associate retiring with growing old and I associate growing old with the end of it all. Maybe it's a lack of faith." Referring to his wife, he says: "we never talk about it (death), we just put it to one side. The conversation we are having now is probably the only conversation I have had or will have about it."

As I read those words, my mind turned to Van Gogh's picture *The Threshold of Eternity*, which I had been studying recently in Frank Elgar's *Van Gogh* (Thames Hudson, 1958, p.217). It depicts with terrible ruthlessness what the prospect of death and the lack of hope meant to the artist. He shows us an old man seated on a chair, his back bowed, his bald head buried in his clenched fists; the bare floorboards and the old battered boots somehow add to the overall picture of despair. It was a vivid illustration of the *Profile* I had been reading.

But the Christian has a prospect which transcends the barrier of death and turns it into a gate of hope. Nor should that hope be too greatly dimmed by the difficulty of expressing the essence of it in clear language. In speaking of such things, we are compelled to use the language of symbol: "there shall be no night there" (Revelation 21:25). Well, we know the dangers which darkness exacerbates and the confidence and freedom which light brings. What the biblical writers are intent on saying is that the God who enters into a covenant-relationship with his children will not have that relationship broken or ended by the incident of the physical dissolution of those children. We cannot believe that we who in this life have enjoyed communion with God will have that communion destroyed by death. That communion, often fragile here, will be closer and stronger there. If in baptism we were buried with Christ, then our "resurrection" will be a partaking in his, and that is of an eternal and incorruptible order. To put it almost crudely: if in this life we have been men and women "in Christ", it is inconceivable that there we shall be "out of him".

There is a confidence in John Bunyan which should be shared by all Christians. Who could put it better than he?

I see myself now at the end of my journey, my toilsome days are ended. I am going now to see that head that was crowned with thorns, and that face that was spit upon for me. I have formerly lived by hearsay and faith; but now I shall go where I shall live by sight, and shall be with him in whose company I delight myself. I have loved to hear my Lord spoken of; and wherever I have seen the print of his shoe in the earth there I have coveted to set my foot too . . . "He has held me, and hath kept me from mine iniquities; yea, my steps hath he strengthened in his way." Now, while he was thus in discourse his countenance changed, his strong man bowed under him; and after he had said, Take me for I come unto thee, he ceased to be seen of them.

Abbé de Tourville put it more succinctly: To die is "to confide oneself hopefully to God" (*Letters of Direction*, p.109).

PRAYERS
OF HOPE

You are my hope, Lord God,
my trust since my childhood.

Psalm 71:5

May God, who is the ground of hope,
fill you with all joy and peace as you
lead the life of faith until, by the power
of the Holy Spirit, you overflow with
hope.

Romans 15:13

I pray that your inward eyes may be enlightened, so that you may know what is the hope to which he calls you . . .

Ephesians 1:18

May our Lord Jesus Christ himself and God our Father, who has shown us such love, and in his grace has given us such unfailing encouragement and so sure a hope, still encourage and strengthen you in every good deed and word.

2 Thessalonians 2:16–17

Almighty and everlasting God, we
most heartily thank thee ... that we
are very members incorporate in the
mystical body of thy Son, which is the
blessed company of all faithful people;
and are also heirs through hope of thy
everlasting kingdom ...

Order of Holy Communion,
Book of Common Prayer

Almighty and everlasting God, give unto us the increase of faith, hope, and charity; and, that we may obtain that which thou dost promise, make us to love that which thou dost command; through Jesus Christ our Lord.

Collect of the 14th Sunday after Trinity,
Book of Common Prayer

In you, Lord, is our hope:
let us not be confounded at the last.

Te Deum

Heavenly Father,
whose blessed Son was revealed
   that he might destroy the works of the devil
and make us the sons of God
and heirs of eternal life:
grant that we, having this hope,
may purify ourselves even as he is pure;
that when he shall appear in power and great glory
we may be made like him
   in his eternal and glorious kingdom;
where he is alive and reigns
   with you and the Holy Spirit,
one God, now and for ever.

Collect of the 8th Sunday before Christmas,
Alternative Service Book, 1980

May we who share Christ's body live
his risen life; we who drink his cup
bring life to others; we whom the Spirit
lights give light to the world. Keep us
firm in the hope you have set before
us, so we and all your children shall be
free, and the whole earth live to praise
your name; through Christ our Lord.

Post-Communion Prayer, Rite A,
Alternative Service Book, 1980

We bless you for our creation, preservation,
   and all the blessings of this life;
but above all for your immeasurable love
in the redemption of the world
   by our Lord Jesus Christ,
for the means of grace, and for the hope of glory.

General Thanksgiving,
Alternative Service Book, 1980

And now we give you thanks for the hope to which you call us in your Son, that following in the faith of all your saints, we may run with perseverance the race that is set before us, and with them receive the unfading crown of glory.

Proper Preface of All Saints' Day,
Alternative Service Book, 1980

Lord Jesus Christ,
Son of the living God,
who at this evening hour rested in
the sepulchre,
and sanctified the grave
to be a bed of hope to your people:
make us so deeply sorry for our sins,
which were the cause of your passion,
that when our bodies lie in the dust,
our souls may live with you;
for with the Father and the Holy Spirit
you live and reign, now and for ever.

Oxford and Cambridge Office Book,
                                    p. 186

O God, the living God, who hast given unto us a living hope by the resurrection of Jesus Christ from the dead: grant that we, being risen with him, may seek the things which are above and be made partakers of the life eternal; through the same Jesus Christ our Lord.

Eternal God, in whom is all our hope
  in life, in death, and to all eternity:
grant that, rejoicing in the eternal life
  which is ours in Christ,
we may face whatever the future holds
  calm and unafraid,
always confident that neither death nor life
  can part us from your love in Jesus Christ
  our Lord.

O Lord our God,
from whom neither life nor death can
separate those who trust in your love,
and whose love holds in its embrace
your children in this world and the
next: so unite us in yourself that in
fellowship with you we may always be
united to our loved ones whether here
or there.

Give us courage, constancy and
hope, through him who died and was
buried and rose again for us,

Jesus Christ our Lord.

William Temple

Christ, whom men saw on the mountain top
   transfigured with the splendour of God:
Christ, whom they saw at thine ascension girt
   about with the light of heaven,
   thy pierced hands stretched out in
   longing over the world:
open our eyes to see thee as thou art.
Help us so to know thee that we may love thee,
   so to love thee that we may grow more like thee,
   so to follow thee that through us others may know
     thee,
   and find in thee their hope, their life, their joy.

From Edmund D. Buxton, *Prayer Plus*, p.62

O Christ our only Saviour, so dwell within us
that we may go forth with
    the light of hope in our eyes,
    and the fire of inspiration in our lives,
    thy word on our lips
    and thy love in our hearts;
  that we may do the will of our heavenly Father
    this day and always.

Almighty and most merciful God, who hast given the Bible to be the revelation of thy great love for us and of thy will and power to save us: grant that our study of it may not be made in vain by the coldness or carelessness of our hearts; but that by it we may be confirmed in penitence,

lifted in hope,

made strong for service

and, above all, filled with the true knowledge of thee and of thy Son our Saviour Jesus Christ.

God, our heavenly Father,
    may we live by faith,
    walk in hope,
    and be renewed in love,
    that the world may reflect your glory,
    and you are all in all.
    Even so; come, Lord Jesus.

Lord, keep me ever near to you.
Let nothing separate me from you,
let nothing keep me back from you.
If I fall, bring me back quickly to you,
and make me hope in you,
trust in you,
love you everlastingly.

E. B. Pusey

Teach me to do thy will, that I may inwardly love thee before all things, with a clean mind and a clean body. For thou art my Maker and my Redeemer, my Help, my Comfort, my Trust, my Hope.

Praise and glory be to thee now, ever and ever, world without end.

Alfred the Great

While I am here on earth let me know you fully;
let my love for you grow deeper here,
so that there I may love you fully.
On earth then I shall have great joy in hope,
and in heaven complete joy in the fulfilment of
my hope.

From the *Proslogion* of St Anselm

Lord, make me an instrument of your peace.
Where there is hatred, let me sow love,
where there is despair, hope . . .

St Francis of Assisi

Lord, may the tongues which "Holy" sang
keep free from all deceiving;
the eyes which saw thy love be bright,
thy blessed hope perceiving.

Liturgy of Malabar

Lord of all hopefulness, Lord of all joy,
whose trust, ever childlike,
    no cares could destroy;
be there at our waking, and give us, we
    pray,
your bliss in our hearts, Lord,
    at the break of the day.

Jan Struther

O God, making all things new:
renew our faith and hope and love.
Renew our wills; that we may serve you
   gladly and watchfully;
renew our delight in your word and worship;
renew our joy in you;
renew our longing that all may come to know you;
renew our desire to serve others,
that so we may walk in the light of your love,
in the power of your Spirit,
now and for evermore. Amen.

Lord, help me to trust you wholly,
for you yourself are the answer to all my need,
    my help in trouble,
    my refuge in danger,
    my strength in temptation,
    my comfort in sorrow,
    my guide in uncertainty,
    my hope in despondency,
    my God, now and for evermore.

O God our loving Father,
   we thank you for all the joy of our humanity,
   but chiefly for the joy of sin forgiven,
   weakness strengthened, victory promised,
   and the hope of life eternal, through
   Jesus Christ our Lord.

George Dawson (abridged and adapted)

We give you thanks, our God and Father,
for all those who have died in the faith of Christ,
for the memory of their words and deeds
    and all they accomplished in their time;
for the joyful hope of reunion with them
    in the world to come;
and for our communion with them now, in your Son,
    Jesus Christ our Lord.

Our Father,
>   give us each day a steady faith,
>   an expectant hope,
>   an outgoing love,
>   through Jesus Christ our Lord.

We have [the hope set before us] ...
as an anchor for our lives, safe and
secure.

Hebrews 6:18–19

Thanks be to God